# CONTENTS

## Our Staff
Publisher: Deng Mayik Atem-USA
Editor in Chief: Kenneth Weene- USA
Senior: Editor Christy White-USA
Editor: Madit D. Ring Yel- USA

### Staff Writers:
Asara Bullen- South Sudan
Adhieu Majok: UK
Achel Tac: USA
Alith Cyer Mayar: South Sudan

### Photographers:
Tino Matoc Deng Mangok: South Sudan
SSOLLYWOOD GLOBAL PRODUCTIONS: South Sudan
Mustafa Khan: South Sudan
Dani' Lee: South Sudan
Chris 4D: South Sudan

Art/Graphics Design-Vertikal Media Group USA/3 E Web Media Manchester UK

The Africa World Books: Australia

### Editorial Offices:
Phoenix, AZ United States
Contact: 1.602-348-2650
Juba, South Sudan
Contact: +21197731641
*www.ramcielmagazine.com*
*info@ramcielmagazine.com*

*Images courtesy of Freepik / wirestock / Racool_studio / pressfoto /*
*suksao / wayhomestudio / jcomp / drobotdean / Hello-Pixel*

*ISBN: 9780645363326*

Ramciel Magazine

Where the Diaspora Meet!

# WELCOME

## -- PUBLISHER'S NOTE --

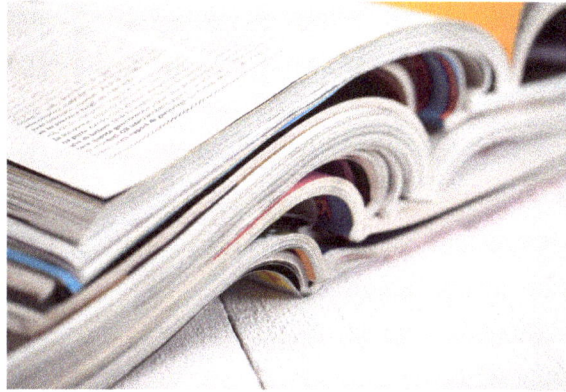

Dear Readers:

Despite the delays caused by Covid-19, we now have our third print edition. During these difficult times and thanks to our online presence, Ramciel Magazine has continued to provide informative stories.

Our third print edition is wide-ranging. We have articles on hydrology, the importance of water; women's rights; mentorship, Run the Race for Peace, claiming our spot on the court, and the celebration of a heroine, Mama Reita Hutson of Phoenix.

I realize that many of our readers spend more time reading online and we continue to offer additional exciting material via your computer. We want to encourage people to engage with stories that pertain to South Sudan on an ongoing basis and not just when or print editions are available.

Please visit our website at www.ramcielmagazine.com. Ramciel Magazine's 2nd print edition is currently available on Amazon.

I am excited to introduce you to Ramciel Social Network which soon be launch, it is where you can discuss and share ideas that are of importance to our people. This new site is found at

Did you know that Ramciel Magazine's fifth anniversary is coming? We are planning to celebrate it April, 2022. Yes, we will be looking back, but more importantly we want to celebrate you, our readers. Please send us your scoops, photos, short stories, poems, and articles. Let us keep the momentum alive.

Once again, thank you so much for being part of the Ramciel Magazine family. Let's all celebrate South Sudan and her independence.

*Deng Mayik Atem*

# RUN THE RACE FOR PEACE

I could find nothing other than toiling
and circulating peace in the crack where I belong.
The emperors have no clothes,
and they are the culprits,
accountable for the cracks,
making our residences sick bays.
As new as this is, they have not been cautious
and subject the innocent to misery and suffering.

Children heading up families increase
and the young give up education to mother siblings.
War injured are resigned to their fate, rotting,
some paralyzed with bullets lodged in their bodies.
Others fled; over 5000 children unaccompanied,
a hard journey under the scorching sun,
unable to find food and water.
What could be worse than meeting the bloody rebels!!

Sacking, the order of the day,
numbers of rebels multiply along tribal perimeters.
What does not kill you, makes you strong!
Our experiences, good or bad, make us who we are.
By overcoming difficulties, we gain strength and maturity.
The trek of tribalism has been circuitous.
Cut it short and make it direct!
Run the race for peace!

*Nyiriak Ramadan*
*April 19th, 2018*

# MENTORSHIP
## IN THE SOUTH SUDAN COMMUNITY

by Acheil Tac

I believe that for our generation to thrive and uplift our nation, we must commit ourselves to helping others the way we help ourselves. We can advance ourselves, but we have to keep in mind that it is essential that we advance our people along with ourselves as individuals. In doing my part, I decided to take the initiative to connect and mentor young South Sudanese Women who play basketball. As a veteran of the game, there were things I knew that I felt I had the opportunity to pass down to the next generation.

Mentorship is important, and not only because of the skills and knowledge one can learn from a mentor, but the personal support they provide that facilitates growth and success. Having the opportunity to acquire an understanding of discipline and being able to learn how to connect with others socially and professionally is key to one's advancement and substantial growth. A lot of our South Sudanese parents often struggle with communication and understanding, and it is understandable how that can sometimes act as a barrier to prevent kids from having crucial and major conversations with their parents -- conversations about college, sports, and scholarships. Growing up as a South Sudanese kid with tough decisions to make out of high school without a mentor, I knew I had to do more to give back to my community and help the kids that were going through what I experienced. The start of my mentorship program started with my sisters. After going through my recruitment process and being so misinformed, I knew that I didn't want another student athlete to go through the same thing. That is when I decided to write and publish my book,

"The Reality Behind the Glamour of College Athletics". I wanted to highlight the reality of college sports as well as educate and inspire a young generation of athletes to want more for themselves. After releasing my book, I wanted to do more. My vision was to create a platform where I would be able to mentor, connect, and provide athletes with the necessary information regarding academics and college athletics.

Sumer 2019, I decided to narrow my scope and start with my own community. Two friends and I gathered contact information and social media accounts of all the South Sudanese girls that were playing high school basketball and reached out to them. Our intention was to help them understand that they were not alone, and to help them realize that there were other girls out there just like them that they could relate to and connect with. Upon collecting all the contact information, we hosted a Zoom meeting. During that meeting we had them introduce themselves so they could get to know one another, and then we answered every question they had lined up. Following the meeting I knew I didn't want it to be a one-time thing. I wanted to keep the connection going and create a space where I could provide them with whatever they needed moving forward. I created a group chat where the girls and I kept up with each other. We used the group chat as a resource and tool to ask questions and provide information. We also used it to check in on each other and make sure everyone was doing well.

Now, you might say that this is not as big or significant as it should be or ought to be, but I beg to differ. When it comes to mentorship, the more intimate it is, the better. The goal is to create relationships with your mentees and be able to influence them positively. When you start adding on without establishing a relationship with the ones you already mentor, the purpose is lost. I believe in quality over quantity. Yes, I would love the opportunity to mentor every South Sudanese kid that I felt needed it, but that is not realistic. For me to be realistic and for my method of mentorship to be effective, I had to start in an area I'm most educated and most influential in. That area is the area of sports and college athletics. Eventually, I plan to branch out and widen my scope, but as of right now I feel as if my community needs me

more. I believe in mentoring and connecting our young generation because I believe they are the future of our great nation. Being able to connect them now communicates numerous things to them.

1. They are not alone
2. Tribe does not matter; we are all one
3. Our goal is the same, so why not help each other?

There is so much more I plan to do in the future, but this is where it starts. My motto has always been inform, mentor, connect, and I hope it continues to grow.

# Dear fellow South Sudanese

By Deng Mayik Atem

I write as a member of the Dinka tribe but, more importantly, as one who loves our country. Recent history has shown that the rivalry for power between the Nuer and Dinka tribes has been destructive for all South Sudanese.

On July 9, 2011, the Republic of South Sudan was born after decades of civil wars and a struggle to establish a common identity as a people. All South Sudanese were jubilant to achieve independence from Sudan; every citizen was excited and looking forward to a brighter future. The new nation was born, and the world was eager to support her. That founding was based on an essential assumption that sovereignty rested with South Sudan people regardless of their ethnicity, tribe, or region. The leaders of a new nation were supposed to establish a system that embraced unity and equity among our citizens. Sadly, that promise has not been met. There is no doubt that the rivalry between Dinka and Nuer has been the monster that has kept our country from moving towards that goal.

The almost ten years since the founding of South Sudan have given a lie to our founding hopes. They have led to violence, continued civil war, corruption, and the wasting of resources. Instead of education, healthcare, new wells in our villages, development of infrastructure, economic development, a sense of common purpose, and increased national prestige, our nation's wealth and effort have gone to empowering a few who rely on weapons, indulgence from Juba, and the helplessness of the many.

More South Sudanese are displaced from their homes than ever. Many continue to take refuge in neighboring countries, and many of us living in the diaspora no longer dream of return. The situation must change. The problem in Juba must be rectified, and a new approach must be taken in the country.

It is time for President Kiir to think seriously about how he will leave the government's power to the people of South Sudan. How does he want this and future generations to remember him? What will his legacy be? We knew that President Kiir is our first president and one of the Republic of South Sudan's founding fathers. That is an outstanding achievement, one worthy of honor. But what will the future say of the culture he leaves behind; of the quality of life, he has brought our people?

Of course, it is easy to say that it is time for a change, that President Kiir should step down and pave the way for an ongoing democratic government. However, if he were to do so, Juba and all South Sudan would be cast back into that never-ending civil strife. The Dinka and Nuer would once again take up arms.

Unless!

I have a suggestion that I believe could serve our nation well and could lead us to national stability. We need a president from among the Bongo, Murle, Kuku, Shilluk, Lou, or other minor tribes. With the power vested in a smaller community,

there would be no sense of threat between the larger tribes. Then we could embrace unity and equity among our people. We could build a coalition that emphasized fairness of sharing and the idea that all regions and tribes could give what they can and that all would receive what they needed. Such a coalition would not do away with political parties and disagreements, but it would encourage alliances that transcended tribal and regional lines.

This may seem strange to say, but we need a president—and, yes, one with real power—who doesn't have some massive, tribal power base. We need a leader whose position and influence are rooted in their ability to build agreements and their willingness to find common ground. I think we need a president who will focus on development instead of catering to their base. I propose that, at least for the short-term, South Sudan will be more governable should a minority be the power base rather than one of the major tribes.

Contact us for Ad Placement
Business Cards $100.00
Leaderboard Banners $200.00

# ADVERTISE WITH

# RAMCIEL MAGAZINE

Sign up before FEB. 2020 to get 20% discount!

# THE INEVITABILITY OF GLOBAL ENERGY TRANSITION AND ITS IMPACT ON THE ECONOMIES OF OIL−DEPENDENT DEVELOPING COUNTRIES

By Madit D. Ring Yel

Does your country rely on oil as the main source of exports and revenue generation? If so, have you thought about a scenario where there is no market for oil? Depending on your interests and profession, you may or may not have entertained the idea of a world where no one wants to buy or sell oil for whatever reasons. Still, if there is ever a time for oil-dependent countries to picture a world without oil, it is today.

It is a fact that oil is a finite resource, and the answer for most oil-producing countries and investors has been to discover and drill for more oil. These efforts have been successful over the years with the advent of efficient technologies, which find and guide oil in new and hard-to-reach places. However, most oil-producing countries have been slow or reluctant to see a world where oil is depleted and out of fashion as a common energy source.

The COVID-19 lockdown effects and the urgency to curb rising CO2 emissions have brought discussions to phase out fossil fuels as energy sources back into the spotlight. From an economic standpoint, COVID-19 lockdowns disrupted global oil markets, bringing oil prices to their lowest in decades at around US$ 18 in April 2020 from about US$ 60 in January (IEA 2020). Oil prices per barrel are back to January 2020 highs of around US$ 60 as of the writing of this article due to promising COVID-19 vaccine distribution and declining infection cases, mainly in developed nations. Nevertheless, some experts warn that oil prices will remain low unless the pandemic is brought under control globally.

The pandemic has given major global economies and multilateral organizations the impetus to adapt and accelerate decarbonization projects to reduce their reliance on fossil fuels and increase the efficiency and adoption of renewable energies such as wind and solar. China, a significant buyer and consumer of fossil fuels for its energy-intensive industrial operations, has pledged to become carbon-neutral by 2060 (IEA 2020). China is currently ramping up its renewable energy capabilities and has the financial means and technical know-how to reach its carbon neutrality goals by the next four decades. Similarly, all major global economies in Europe and North America have made carbon neutrality pledges, including their commitment to the more multilateral Paris Climate accord, which has 196 signatories and aims at bringing global warming to an average of 1.5 degrees celsius or less in the next few decades.

The impact of COVID-19 disruptions on oil prices and the need to save the world from global warming have significant economic and social implications on oil-dependent developing countries, especially those in Africa and the Middle

East. If you are still reading this article (I hope you are) and assuming you are South Sudanese, you might now be wondering: where does South Sudan fit in this conversation?

At the beginning of this article, I posed two questions about whether your country relies on oil exports and revenue and whether you have thought of a future scenario where there is no willing buyer and seller of your oil. The first question applies to South Sudan as an oil-dependent developing country. As for the second question, it is no longer a scenario. It is a fact, and the question is not if there will ever be no market for oil, but when.

Commodity experts and analysts differ on the timing when oil is irrelevant, both as a viable financial investment where prices are so low it is not worth investing in and when countries no longer use it as a source of energy due to $CO_2$ emission concerns and regulations. However, it is estimated that oil prices will range from US$ 100-200 per barrel in the next few years before its eventual decline in the 2040s onward.

At the current production levels and global oil prices, South Sudan already faces many challenges to produce and export enough oil to meet its growing national fiscal needs. Currently, South Sudan has around 170,000-180,000 b/d compared to about 300,000 b/d in 2011 (EIA 2019). This reduction in production levels is mainly attributed to disruptions caused by subsequent civil unrest and lack of technical capacities. Secondly, we know that South Sudan refines and exports its oil through Sudan by paying a certain percentage from oil revenues and relies on some Middle Eastern and Asian countries for oil exports.

Whether South Sudan will capitalize on the potential oil price increases in the short- and medium-term remains to be seen. But the pressing and more urgent questions are: What will happen to South Sudan and Sudan's fiscal and macro-economic well-being when oil revenue dries out due to the changing global energy transition?

The answer might be obvious depending on viable alternative economic sectors in South Sudan from which export revenues can be extracted: agriculture and livestock, other minerals like gold, efficient tax collection, tourism development, among others. But developing and removing export revenue from these alternative economic sectors will require the government to exercise immense prudence with public financial management, plans to create alternative economic sectors including human capital, and prepare for a post-oil economy in South Sudan.

Anything short of severe political will and strategies to diversify away from relying on oil as a main source of income will deprive South Sudan of a much-needed development following decades of conflicts and put the country in a cycle of poverty and civil unrest.

*Madit D. Ring Yel is a South Sudanese professional with experience and interests in business, economics, and development. He holds bachelor's in Business, Economics and a master's in Global Affairs and Management. You can connect with the author on LinkedIn and Twitter @ MaditYel*

# Women's Empowerment

*A conversation with Ms. Viola Riak, South Sudanese Child Activist*

**RM:** Tell us about yourself.

**VR:** Well, I will tell you about the Viola Aluel that people don't know.

I come from a polygamous family; my mother is the second wife of five. From my mother, I am the last born and the only girl to three brothers. Since I was six years old, I and my two older brothers were single-handedly raised by mother.

During my second year of university I got pregnant and, by the time I was nineteen, I became a mother to my daughter who is now sixteen.

My mother supported me financially and emotionally; she went as far as getting a nanny to take care of my child so that I could go back to university and finish my degree.

Today I am a married woman blessed with three children (two daughters and one son), and I hold a master's degree from one of the best universities in Africa

**RM:** Who is your role model?

**VR:** My mother. This woman has seen it all -- from her father being killed as she watched, having to drop out of school to help her mother raise her siblings, being forced to marry a man she didn't love at nineteen, getting divorced in her early twenties, being separated from her seven year old first born, and becoming a second wife in her late twenties.

My mother's life experience shaped me into who I am today. She is the reason why I advocate against gender-based violence, including all harmful traditional practices such as forced child marriages. Using my life as a real example, when I was only six years old, my parents separated. I saw how my mother struggled to provide for us. With only an intermediate certificate, she ensured all our basic needs were cared for. Sometimes I look back and imagined what my life would have been if my mother had not been educated, if she wasn't empowered?

**RM:** What is women empowerment?

**VR:** Women empowerment is all about equipping and giving opportunities such as education, employment and skills that enable women determine their lives, overcome life challenges and being able to make their own decisions such as when to marry, whom to marry, including when to walk away from toxic and abusive marriages.

Could you briefly talk about a few barriers hindering women's empowerment in South Sudan?

South Sudan is a patriarchal society which is a leading cause in persistent gender inequalities in the form of gender norms and beliefs that treat men and boys as superior to women and girls. Women and girls continue to be treated as secondary citizens with little status in the socio-cultural fabric of the society.

Women attain low levels of education, and access to resources for women and girls are limited. The social roles that hinder women from utilizing their full potential, prevalent child marriage, low formal labour market participation, lack of space for autonomous decision making even in regards to their own bodies and reproductive health, low participation in decision making, etc.

**RM:** Why is women's empowerment important for a country like South Sudan?

**VR:** Women's empowerment is important for the realization of gender equality as granted in the bill of rights of our constitution. Women and girls constitute about 48% of the South Sudan population, leaving them behind will hinder the achievement of sustainable development in our country.

Here's a real example. Imagine a family where the husband and wife are both educated and employed. This is a family that will be able to have a good living including good shelter, health care, education and security.

**RM:** What does South Sudan need to achieve women's empowerment and gender equality?

**VR:** The South Sudan constitution, and various policies and strategies, guarantee women, men, girls and boys equal rights without discrimination. The major problem we are facing in this country is reinforcement of these laws and policies. Customary laws that discriminate toward women and girls are still being highly reinforced and practiced. If we are to realize gender equality, Government must ensure all legal frameworks are reinforced with strict punishments for those that violate these laws and policies.

**RM:** Thank you for your time Ms. Riak.

*Ms. Viola Riak is a Social Scientist and Gender Activist from South Sudan. She is currently a UNFPA Gender Analyst based in Juba. She has over 8 years' experience in peacebuilding, conflict resolution/transformation, and gender equality. Ms. Riak is a champion on prevention and response to gender-based violence including child marriage in South Sudan. She is a strong advocate on issues of sexual reproductive health services, including the right to access family planning. Ms. Riak holds a Master of Social Sciences in Social Development from the University of Cape Town (UCT) and a Bachelor of Arts in Community Development from Daystar University.*

# ATHIEIDA MEDIA GROUP
## Redefining Your Brand

# THE SCOPE OF WHAT WE DO...

**AMG** *CONDUCTS INNOVATIVE, CREATIVE & QUALITY MEDIA PRODUCTIONS IN VARIOUS ASPECTS OF ADVERTISEMENTS:*

1. NEWSPAPERS
2. MAGAZINES
3. PROFESSIONAL PHOTOGRAPHY
4. GRAPHIC DESIGNINGS
5. PUBLICATIONS AND WRITTEN TEXT- (DOCUMENTS)
6. RADIO COVERAGE ACROSS MEDIA CHANNELS

*We also support our client's organization's media relations efforts after the media productions.

*We also conduct Promotional activities for fast-moving consumer goods, using a professional team. We do these using Exhibitions, Activations, Events, Sales Promotions, and Market Seeding.

*We have a creative team that designs merchandise with the help of our PR department that is concerned with the public image of our existing partners and clients.

# Bakhita Nyanyal Nhial Biel

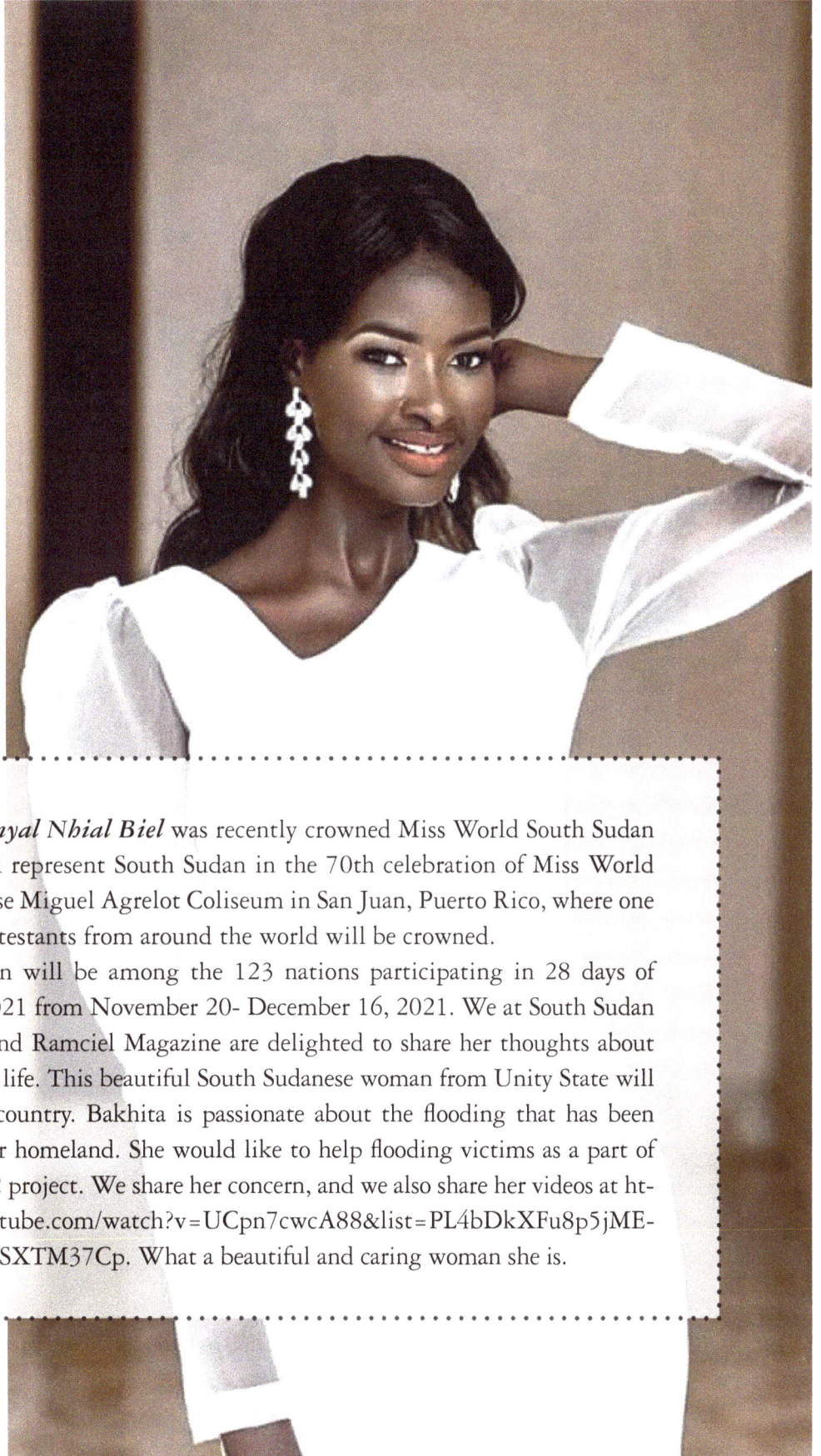

*Bakhita Nyanyal Nhial Biel* was recently crowned Miss World South Sudan 2021. She will represent South Sudan in the 70th celebration of Miss World 2021 at the Jose Miguel Agrelot Coliseum in San Juan, Puerto Rico, where one of the 123 contestants from around the world will be crowned.

South Sudan will be among the 123 nations participating in 28 days of Miss World 2021 from November 20- December 16, 2021. We at South Sudan Music Video and Ramciel Magazine are delighted to share her thoughts about her family and life. This beautiful South Sudanese woman from Unity State will represent our country. Bakhita is passionate about the flooding that has been devastating our homeland. She would like to help flooding victims as a part of her 2021-2022 project. We share her concern, and we also share her videos at https://www.youtube.com/watch?v=UCpn7cwcA88&list=PL4bDkXFu8p5jME--w1OYGli4PySXTM37Cp. What a beautiful and caring woman she is.

# A Conversation with Honorable Tor Deng Mawien

By Ramciel Magazine's Deng Mayik Atem, Juba, South Sudan, August 22-23, 2021.

*Disclaimer: The opinions expressed in this interview with Honorable Tor Deng Mawien are his own words and do not reflect the view of the Ramciel Magazine.*

Honorable Tor served as Governor of Warrap State, Deputy Speaker of the South Sudan Legislative Assembly, and Advisor to President Salva Kiir on decentralization.

**RM:** Who is Tor Deng Mawien, and when did you join politics?

**HTDM:** I joined the government in 1998 as a minister of Health in what was then Warrap State. Then, in 2000, I was relieved of office and returned to the NCP party's general headquarters in the specialized secretarial office for political and organization. I worked there until 2001. Then, in 2001, I was appointed again as deputy governor and minister of the Infrastructure of Warrap State. Comrade Machar Achiek Adaria was from Tonj, and I was his deputy. Then, in 2002, he (Machar) was relieved from the office, and I was designated governor, and then I was relieved. But Deng Mawien was the next appointed governor of Warrap State. He and I share names, but we are not related. He is from Kuacjok.

In 2004, I was appointed again as a full governor of Warrap State through 2005 during the six-month interim period of C.P.A. and before the Interim Period. The late Dr. John Garang decided to relieve all the governors of the ten states. He replaced us with political supervisors or caretaker governors except for General Clement Wani Kanga of Central Equatoria.

In 2005, I was appointed deputy speaker, although the position of deputy speaker was not mentioned in the C.P.A. This is because there wasn't such a position in the C.P.A. But the SPLM, and because of their partnership with the National Congress Party, agreed to that position.

**RM:** What motivated you personally to go into politics?

**HTDM:** What motivated me is a long history. When we were in a senior secondary school in 1976, we were young recruits of the Sudan Communist Party. At that time, Dr. Yusuf Bashar was academic secretary. When it came to allocating chances or opportunities for learning abroad, especially scholarships to attend schools abroad, he always focused on northerners by saying southerners are born communists and, therefore, don't need much training in communist ideologies. So, I told him, Dr. Yusuf, "Doctrine must go hand-in-hand with knowledge. Yes, I am a communist, but I am not a doctor, lawyer, or engineer. I needed the training to have the skill to put together with the ideology to have a position in the community and talk to the people like they would say Doctor X was here treating people. They will be happy, and if they are so glad, people will listen to you."

So, we needed to receive equal opportunity as Sudanese in general. Excluding us was something we saw as segregation and discrimination.

When this thing continued, we had no choice but to defect from the Sudan Communist Party, and we formed our party in South Sudan. We called it "NAM," the Nationalists Action Movement. A comrade led it from Western Equatoria, Ustaz Tarestizeo Ahmed. Tarestizeo Ahmed, I and Edward Lino, Santo Madison, Bol Makeng Yuol, currently in the SPLM Secretariat, and even Samuel Gai Tut were our members. We were active and were the ones who made ready the ground for the Unity Movement that created the mutiny, especially among the youths who like to strike.

We led protests against the drawing of a new border between the North and the south of Sudan. The drawing of those borders had created a problem that we are still facing today. Now, we still have a conflict of the contesting areas between North and south. Also, we led a strike and demonstrations against Nimeiry's decision to make *kacha* or deportation of those who came to stay in Khartoum, especially Southerners. Especially he enacted the September Law (Islamic Sharia). His administration started to deport Darfurians, South Sudanese, and others, and those allowed to stay in the capital of Khartoum were always accused of being a thief, and their hands were chopped off.

Also, we struck because of the oil being described as some hundred kilometers south of Khartoum, and this is the oil in Bentiu that they are describing. We also led the strike against the Jonglei Canal. I was a political activist during my youth, and I am a career politician.

**RM:** Do you think that South Sudan will survive and become a viable nation?

**HTDM:** Yes. And well, this time of difficulty is a natural thing. Every Country in the world passed through tough times or hurdles. This tribulate; each Country went through such a thing, even the United States went through the same situation. The American Civil War was called a war for unity. When the southern states were defeated, that brought what the United States is now. So, the same thing is what we are undergoing currently, but it is not permanent. It will go away.

South Sudan is endowed with many resources, including animals, soil, urban land, gold, gas, uranium, fishery, agriculture, and more. When South Sudan successfully utilizes its mineral resources and has developed well-planned agriculture, not only will our country be standing on its feet, but it will be the breadbasket of the region, if not the whole continent of Africa.

**RM:** Is there a trick to get Dinka and Nuer to work together?

**HTDM:** These are all divisive ideas; when you encourage the other tribes to unite against the Dinka and Nuer, you encourage tribal and regional divisions. If you single out the two tribes, Dinka and Nuer, out of the sixty-four, what would be the guarantee the sixty-two will not gang up against both Dinka and Nuer? What makes you think they will be in harmony without Dinka and Nuer? They will still complain, especially the minor tribes, about the domination of the others; for example, in Equatoria, about the Zande and Topasa because those are the most prominent tribes.

Then there is the question of what a tribe is. Here in Juba, it is assumed that Bari is a big group. They are big because of what is called "the Bari speaking group." Bari-speaking groups are not all Bari; for instance, Mundari is an independent tribe, but they speak a Bari language. When you subtract the Bari speaking group from the Bari tribe, then the tribe is a little one.

The best way forward is to work together for the peaceful coexistence of these sixty-four tribes, and to build a spirit of brotherhood and sisterhood is the best option than building blocks or highlands of tribes to fight each other.

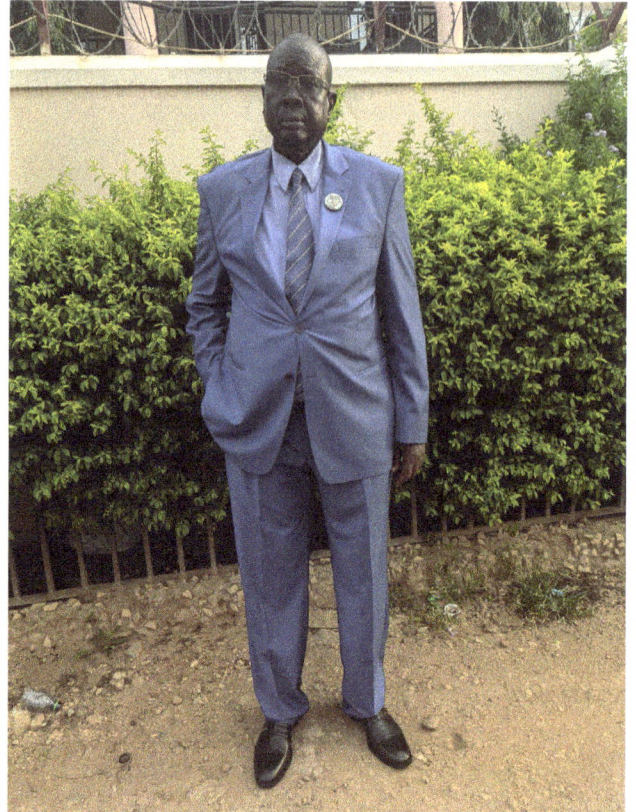

**RM:** What are a few of the landmarks in our nation's short history that you would like to draw attention to? Which leaders do you want to remind us to celebrate?

**HTDM:** 1800s, Aliab revolution leaders such as Kon Anok Ngengeer. 1900s, Ali Abdellah Thiep staged a resistance against Colonizers.

Nuer Spiritual leader's son Aguak Ngundeng brought down a helicopter by a Boloong (wooden- atoal). The Britons were surprised what sort of weapon was used by the Nuer warriors. Aguek Ngundeng climates up the tree, and he knocks down the plane. That weapon used to bring down the Helicopter is now kept in the British archive.

In Western Equatoria: King Gbudwe of Azande staged a resistance, and he was fought by the two giant nations of France and the British before he was defeated.

**1950s.** those of Madut Chan and the soldier's rebellion of 1955 were pure soldiers without much support from ordinary citizens.

**1960s,** those of William Deng Nhial, Aggrey Jaden, Father Santurino, Joseph Oduho, Bona Malwal,

Abel Alier, Joseph Lagu, Martin Majier Gai, Peter Gatkuoth

**Anya Anya one,** those of Abur Nhial-Matoug, Albino Akol Akol, of course of the Salva Kiir, John Garang was young and their foot soldiers.

SPLA/M 1983-2005, those of Dr. John Garang, Kuerbino Kuanyin Bol, William Nyuon, Arok Thon Arok, Salva Kiir, and others. They established the Movement, fought bravely, and negotiated the peace deal successfully to the interest of the South Sudanese citizens by creating a forum that ended the war once and for all between the North and South by calling for Self-Determination in a Machakos Protocol. The C.P.A. was concluded in Naivasha in 2005, the leader of the Movement (SPLA/M), Dr. John Garang, suddenly died in a helicopter crash when he was coming from Kampala to the New Site in South Sudan.

Salva Kiir Mayardit took the banner, and Salva Kiir proved to be honest and brave, patriotic South Sudanese, but the Arabs and not the Arabs in the North, but the Arabs in the Arab world tried many ways to keep Sudan as one Country. Those of late Muammar Gaddafi, King of Saudi Arabian, Qatar, and Kuwait, were helping northerners convince Southerners to keep and maintain the unity of Sudan and refrain from the division of the Country. But Salva Kiir consistently and persistently stood his ground by saying, only you people, I am just only a guard to guard the implementation of the peace agreement, and the final say is with the people of South Sudan. But I want to tell you, people, that the decision is not mine, my conclusion is only one come the 9th of January 2011, and the referendum is not conducted and the Sunrise in the morning up to the Sunset and the referenda is not started, what will happen, I will not be responsible, so that statement made the northerners to accept the conduction of the referendum because the statement mean there will be a war. So Salva Kiir managed to manage the difficult period, which was the interim period of six years. He managed wisely, carefully, and bravely with all the odds with the North; he endured very patiently enough because his eye was on the referendum. He never minded any other things, and he was only eyeing the referendum, and he raised the flag of the new nation and was the one who proclaimed the independence of the new Republic and pulled down the then the flag of Sudan. He held and gave it to President Omer el Bashir, and he raised the new banner of now-independent South Sudan. So, he manages a big and most significant landmark that could be attributed to him.

Because Salva Kiir and the independence of South Sudan are inseparable, he fought two civil wars, and he never enjoyed his youthfulness, or he enjoyed his marriage life, and even now, he is not enjoying his old age. But he had devoted all his lifetime to the case of South Sudan. So, he is outstanding, like the late William Deng Nhial.

**RM:** Is Salva Kiir a father of the nation?

**HTDM:** Of course, he's the father of the nation. He who raised the flag and proclaimed the Country's independence is the father and founder of the nation? Dr. John Garang founded the Movement. However, the person who realized the country, who brought it to reality, is Salva Kiir.

**RM:** How was your working relationship with both Presidents Salva Kiir and President Bashir? Some people say that you are the most potent presidential advisor to President Kiir and that nothing goes to him without stopping on your desk. They say that you are the determining factor regarding how things are coordinated around President Kiir. Is this true?

**HTDM:** You cannot prevent people from thinking whether it is a reality or not, but my relation with Kiir is cordial. Kiir was the one who conceded when President Bashir asked him that he wanted the deputy speaker of the South Sudan Legislative Assembly to be allocated to the National Congress Party. And Bashir had a candidate for the position; his name was Tor Deng Mawien. "Do you know him?" He asked Kiir.

H.E. TOR DENG MAWIEN
Governor of Warrap State
AKON – 16.11.2008

in South Sudan, and the SPLM members, which was because of me. I managed to bring everyone together, and we discussed any bill brought to benefit the people of South Sudan. Of course, there was a lot of tension at that time, and it was a challenging time. The SPLA soldiers were eyeing us as the enemies and traitors who fought against them. Now we were to share power with them, but I tried my best to make them feel that we were their brothers and sisters and not their enemies. That was one of the achievements in my working relationship with president Kiir and others in South Sudan, especially in the South Sudan Legislative Assembly.

RM: Are you and Salva Kiir related?

HTDM: Yes. Of course, we are cousins, and we are from the same area.

RM: Reconciliation and healing: If reconciliation was conducted right after South Sudan's independence, could it have helped prevent the conflict?

HTDM: Absolutely! Reconciliation and healing were some of the most important provisions of the C.P.A. It was supposed to be conducted before the secession of South Sudan. It was going to be the reconciliation and the healing of the whole Country of Sudan.

What prevented it from being conducted at that time was the war in Darfur. You cannot make reconciliation and healing in one part of the Country while the other is bleeding? So, the process was postponed until the case of Darfur was settled, when Sudan was free from any conflict.

Unfortunately, it didn't happen until the referendum came, and the South voted overwhelmingly for independence. Independence was proclaimed, so now it became reconciling among South Sudanese, some of whom did bad things against our people during the struggle. For instance, the 1991 incident/mutiny by Dr. Riek Machar, Dr. Lam Akol, and company. They defected from the Movement.

"Yes. I know him. Tor Deng Mawien and I came from the same area," President Kiir responded.

Then Bashir asked him again, "Will you work with him?"

"Yes, why not?" Kiir agreed. Had Salva Kiir refused, I would not have been the deputy speaker of the South Sudan Legislative Assembly. After I resigned from the NCP, he saw how I managed the partnership and the coalition between the SPLM and the NCP, how I ordered it.

I asked the South Sudanese members of the NCP, which came first, South Sudan or the political party we belonged to? Every one of them agreed with me that South Sudan came first. We were born in South Sudan; all our ancestors were born and died in the land of South Sudan, and now what was dividing us was just different opinions because some of us wanted to join the NCP, and some were SPLM members. But we belong to the same land, and we are one people at the end of the day. Therefore, in our work in the Assembly, we must work as a group, not as opposites. We were like one body in the Assembly, the NCP members

In late 2011, after the Proclamation of Independence, the committee was formed headed by Dr. Riek Machar, then vice president of the Republic, and I was his deputy. The committee was big enough, and we were planning to invite some prominent peace award holders like Bishop Tutu and other leaders or peacemakers in the world. So, we extended them the invitations.

But what happened in due course of this, Dr. Riek had a different motive altogether. He was acting as if he was doing reconciliation, but he was aiming at two things: he was after or pursuing the forgiveness of Bor people because of the massacre he committed in 1991 in Bor. He wanted Bor people to forgive him, and that's what he meant by the reconciliation. His goal for the reconciliation and healing was for him to come back as a clean person in the eyes of the South Sudanese such that he could run to be the President of the country when the election came.

**RM:** Why was it a bad idea for Dr. Riek to have a desire to run for the presidency? After all, he has every right to run for the President of South Sudan.

**HTDM:** Well, he should have done it differently. First of all, it would have been good to make a comprehensive peace, reconciliation, and healing of all South Sudanese people. We should talk, listen, and forgive each other and go back to coexisting and brotherhood. Then he can make his political agenda clear, but he should not have sandwiched his political motive along with this noble program of reconciliation and healing. Unfortunately, when people knew what he was aiming at, the committee was dissolved. It led to his dismissal as vice president of South Sudan, which led to the fighting in December 2013.

What Riek wanted was to take over power quickly; he wanted a shortcut because he became impatient. He thought that at the time, Nuer Militias were the majority in the army. After General Paulino Matiop, his rival was gone, Dr. Riek Machar became the lone leader in the Nuer community.

Besides the army, many Nuer were in organized forces such as police, wildlife, Army, Prison ward, and National Security. He thought that people would come out and stage a coup by chasing away the Dinka and that with the Dinka gone, the other tribes would not resist.

It is only the Dinka who will withstand, but what Riek thought wasn't correct. The opposite happened. The majority of the Nuer on whom he was depending were defeated, and they ran away.

People went to him and asked him to negotiate and address the grudges and inconveniences amicably and peacefully. These were political issues, and they needed to be settled politically and not by force. He accepted that request, which led to the signing of the Compromise Agreement in 2015. But Dr. Riek delayed coming to Juba so that the national unity government couldn't be formed. Instead, in 2016, he tried again to make a palace coup, which led to the fight in J1. So many young people died, especially on his side. So many soldiers lost their lives. He went back again to the bush.

Now he has again been brought back, and we don't know what's in his mind? But hopefully, he will fully implement the recently Revitalized Agreement of Resolution of the Conflict in South Sudan.

**RM:** Perhaps you can tell us a bit about the 1947 Juba Conference compared to the 2005 Comprehensive Peace Agreement (C.P.A.). Primarily, looking back to the conference of 1947, could things have worked out differently at the conference? What is your thought?

**HTDM:** Well, the 1947 Juba Conference was way different than the 2005 C.P.A.

There was no balance in the 1947 Juba Conference because South Sudanese were negotiating with the highly skilled Arab northerners. However, compared to the 2005 Naivasha negotiation, South Sudanese were highly confident, if not superior, to their northern counterparts.

Although the Northerners had tried to do the same tactics that were done in the 1947 Juba conference, it did not work well because there was balance in the standard, especially the educational background, which was not existing with our people in 1947. In the negotiations that led to the signing of the C.P.A., the Arabs were surprised by the capacity of the South Sudanese intellectuals when they reached the agreement on wealth sharing, especially the sharing of the oil revenues, primarily produced in the Southern part the Country.

This notion of sharing the oil revenue fifty-fifty with Southern Sudan getting 50% and the rest of the Country with 50% wasn't received well by the northern leaders and even the ordinary people. People protested that how come a part of a country be given fifty percent of the oil revenues and the large part comprised of the Central, East, north, and western Sudan are given fifty percent? So, I and Professor Moses Machar were called to a meeting at the Graduate Club or in Arabic it is called "Nadia Karahrachgen." It is one of the historical sites where those of Ali Abdellah-Thiep started the white banner to resistance against the colonial rule, and we were there to meet the Sudanese government's negotiating team who just returned from the peace negotiations in Naivasha, Kenya.

The negotiating team was called to enlighten people about how they reached and accepted such a deal with the Rebels, especially the wealth-sharing protocol. So, one of the negotiators said, ha, you guys are still holding the mentality of 1947, but today's Junubian are pretty different from Southerners of 1947. The Southerners are even teaching us about certain things about this oil. Items which we were not prepared for, they brought them up during the negotiations. So, don't assume that it is more accessible work than we are doing now. So that's why I concluded that there was no balance if you compare 1947 and 2005, especially in the early 2000s when the conventional negotiation started and led to the signing of the C.P.A. in 2005. The negotiation was well balanced; South Sudanese were well informed about everything, and they delivered very well.

**RM:** Let's talk about the political theory behind our nation and the Republic of South Sudan Constitution. How might the constitution be altered to better deal with tribal and regional differences? Since you were a part of the reviewing committee, what have you done to address the issues raised by certain quarters in South Sudan regarding federalism? People want a system of federalism. What kind of a governance system do we have in South Sudan?

**HTDM:** Well, the definition of South Sudan is that it is constitutionally territorial comprised of ten states in the first interim constitution 2005, and again we amended in 2005 up to the Proclamation of Independence.

On the 9th of July 2011, the interim constitution was maintained because any government's main objectives or goals are to keep territorial integrity and the unity of the people. Adopting this democratic, decentralized system of governance was meant to address this question of nationalities. These nationalities' dialects are recognized and upgraded to be languages regardless of how small or more significant the tribe is, so their cultures could be developed such that no one culture can be dominant; that's also why English was chosen to be the official national language of South Sudan because we want the language that brings people together. So, instead of saying let us introduce Dinka, Nuer, Bari, or any other language of South Sudan. In Malaysia, for example, they went the other way. Even though there are different ethnicities in the county, Malaysian is the official language. In Uganda, Buganda is a tribe, and its language is the official language being spoken countrywide (besides Kiswahili/Swahili). The same thing in India, its official language, is Hindi, although millions don't say it. Of course, in India, English is also an official language.

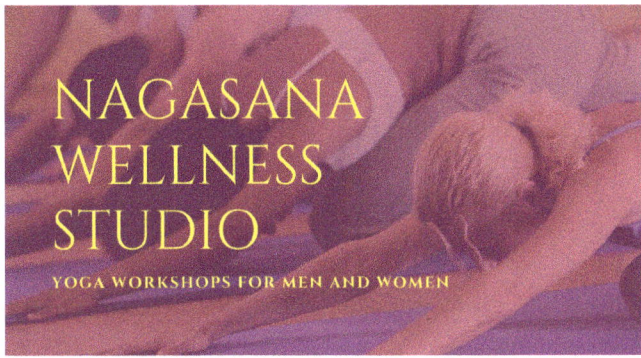

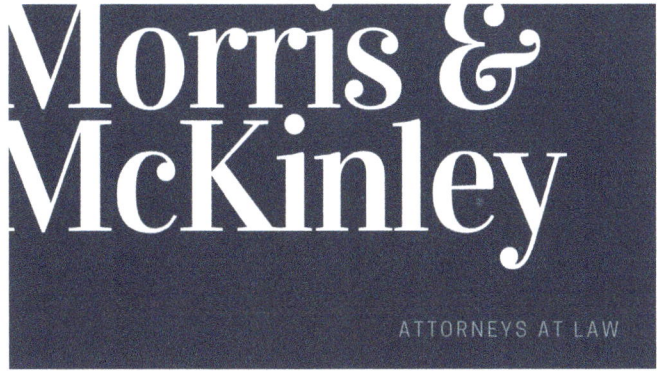

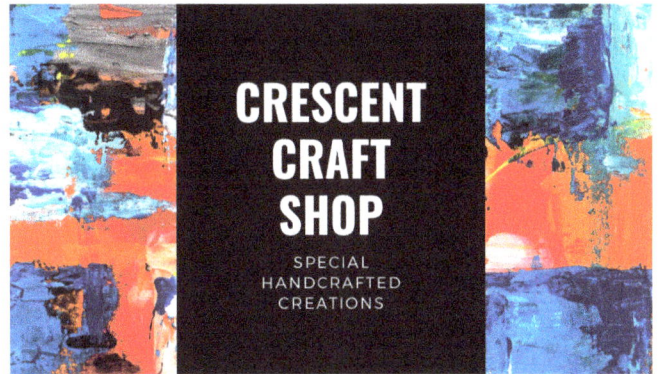

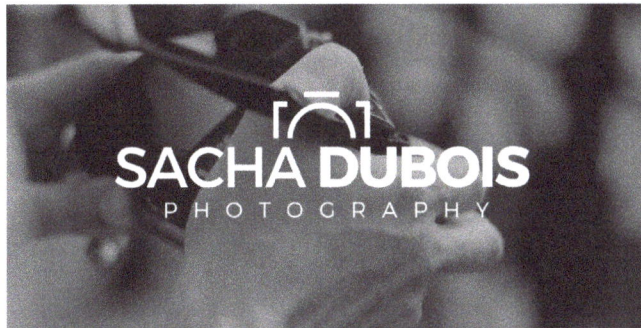

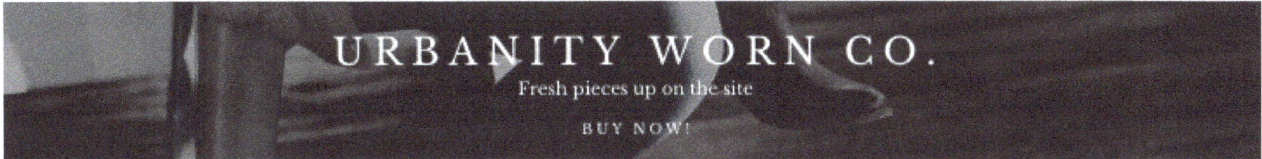

**RM:** This will lead us to a follow-up question regarding recent development from the Western Bahr el Ghazal state where Governor Mayar Achor declared that Lou should be the official name for the Jur-Chol people and that Jurchol was a nickname given to the Lou people by their neighbors, the Dinka. Should their wish be recognized by the government of South Sudan? What is your take on that?

**HTDM:** This question of tribalism and how it should be addressed. Well, it had already been addressed with the things cherished in the constitution and the main thing now when it comes to political decentralization. Each one of the states elects their governor; they select their member of the state of Assembly. They were supposed to elect their counties commissioners, but when the election came in 2010, it stopped only at the state level and wasn't carried down to the county level. So next time it will be administrated at the county level. So, the county commissioners will no longer be appointed by the states' governors. The commissioners will be elected by their constituents just like the governors are elected the whole state. So that commissioners will have space there can work without fear of being removed by the governor. An elected official is answerable to the people who elected them, but the commissioners will cooperate and coordinate with the governors.

When it comes to this question, rather the "Jur-Chol of Wau should be called L.O.U. or not."

This took us a very long debate; first of all, we told them that point-blank historically, we were already being called Jurchol, which you people accepted. When they colonized, the Turks or Egyptians ruled. In 1889, the Ango-Egyptians came and defeated Mahdist and Sudan fell under Anglo-Egyptian Condominium rule. At that time, they were also called Jur-chol. When the British divided South Sudan into three provinces of Bahr El Ghazal, Equatoria, and Upper Nile, they created districts within these provinces. One of the districts of Bahr el Ghazal is called Jur River District. The Jur River District, which is still established in Wau, comprises non-Jur people. That district includes Tonj and Gogrial, the two areas put together and were named Jur River District. So, when they tried to bring it up here in the National Legislative Assembly, we told them it was not valid. We didn't name the area Jur-Chol. We are the citizens of the Jur River District, and we are not Jurs, but we accepted it. Now, you want to change and call it Lou District. Who gave this river to be yours? It was a colonizer who gave this name Jur, and it is God-given because we are the inhabitants of the area along the bank of the river and second to that when it comes to this name Lou, it is not only for Jur alone, even the Dinka and Nuer are included. The Lou mean Nilotics, especially the tribe along the river Nile. Even here in Equatoria, we have Acholi, and even Acholi of Uganda are part of the Lou tribe plus the Lou of Kenya.

**RM:** Development in South Sudan: There have been no ambitious recent projects except the current Bor-Road, which is Chinese investment in our Infrastructure. For a while, the Chinese have been doing their part. Are Americans and Westerners also welcome to participate and invest in South Sudan? Do you think South Sudan has enough resources to keep other countries, especially China, the United States, and perhaps the European Union, involved in our nation's development?

HTDM: The development opportunities are vast, and it can accommodate as many as want to take part. The only problem is that the investments of westerners, Europeans, and Northern Americans—particularly the United States—are highly connected with their governments; and it is the policy of their governments that they their investments come with certain preconditions, preconditions such as human rights, democracy, and many other things.

These things couldn't be done overnight; they needed a slow and gradual process. Young nations couldn't be fully-blown democratic drastically. They go through so many hurdles until they become fully aware, and awareness is essential. Although our people have their natural democratic ways of electing or selecting their chiefs, they don't vote using the ballot box. Anyone contesting for the chieftain comes up and stands on a line, his opponent on another line. Their supporters line up behind the candidate of their choice, and people are counted. He who gets the majority of members becomes the chief of his community. It is a direct democracy.

Our disagreement with the westerners and the United States, in particular, is not our creation; it is their creation. During the peace negotiations, our negotiating team, led by late Dr. John Garang, said all the oil or petroleum contracts signed by the Khartoum government with the Chinese ought to be canceled. We will make new concessions as the owner of the resources, but the Americans themselves refused and advised South Sudan not to chase away the Chinese.

But the South Sudanese knew that the Chinese were arming the Khartoum government during the conflicts. Even when Sudan was under the arms embargo sanction, the Chinese continued to supply the Sudanese army with the latest weapons. Their weapons devastated South Sudan during the Civil War. Therefore, the Chinese company doesn't deserve to continue drilling for oil in South Sudan. But the Americans have said, "No, you only go and review those contracts with the Chinese. You read the arrangements and make sure you know the contents of those contracts and leave until expired and make Chinese your friends."

We agreed to follow the Americans' advice. Now they are charging that we favor China because our relationship with China is effective because of three things:

Americans think we favored the Chinese and that we sidelined them and forgot about their support during back days. This is what they are telling us. But we are telling Americans that the door is open to allow your people to come if you act like the Chinese. Because the Chinese don't get involved in any country's internal affairs. The Chinese always come with one particular aim, to invest. But the Americans come with the mentality; they want to share power with the government by dictating things from the government. But we want to execute certain things for ourselves. We shouldn't be waiting for America to do what they want us to do first while we are hungry, sick, we want education. You want us to be a fully democratic state when we have this high illiteracy rate in South Sudan and the anger. We still have so many challenges. We don't even have an economy. We don't have big schemes to produce some cash crops for domestic consumption with a subsistence economy. If there is a surplus, it will be taken to the world market to bring hard currencies to develop our economy further. That is why we favored the Chinese, and we were never given a level ground to compete with the Chinese. Still, we told them no, our environment is already marked for all of you, and you should come. It is not just the oil and gas production industry alone. There are other areas; if you go to the western Bahr el Ghazal, you can find uranium, gold in Kapoeta, agriculture, where you can grow coffee and tea.

Second, Islam will penetrate Africa from the door, which is South Sudan. South Sudan is the door to block Islam away. So, we tell the Americans that the whole of western African is predominately Islam. Almost every nation in the West has the highest Muslim population. Forget North African; they are already Arab and Islamic countries. North Africa is a different case, and back in East Africa here, for instance, Somalia is almost 100% Islamic.

Tell us which country doesn't have a Muslim population; even in Vatican City, Muslim communities are probably there. There may be some Muslim workers and representatives.

So, Islam is a wave that could not be blocked by South Sudan alone. We said that we would not allow radical Islam to enter South Sudan, but moderate Muslims can; we provide in our constitution the respect of all religions and traditional believers.

# ELIZABETH CONVENIENT STORE AND HAIR BRAIDING

## SO MUCH MORE!

**4935 W Glendale Ave, Glendale, AZ 85301**
**(623) 486-2974**

Clothes, Food, Beauty Items, Something for your home!  Hair Braiding and more...Come by and see us.

RM: Are you interested in how our Country's culture changes, especially in our young people's tastes? Do you have some favorite musicians and other South Sudanese artists you recommend? How about authors?

HTDM: Frankly speaking, I am not happy with the way our young generation is conducting themselves. They are copying everything from the West and especially from East Africa without a context. So, they have diluted our cultures, especially the way our people dress. The way they make their hair! All young look mad in the eye of the elders, and this is quite a surprise. The way they dance tells you that our own culture has been disowned. Even our own languages/mother-tongues are lacking, although we are trying here.

We worried about your kids, especially you people in the Diaspora, because we thought you were the people with better chances in the Western World to get an education, to be educated, and come back home to your country and develop your own country and enjoy it. But now we are hearing discouraging news that most young people are getting into all those destructive behaviors, which worry us so much. So, our cultures are being endangered.

RM: The world has changed a great deal in the years since you first became involved in the politics of Sudan. One of the most significant changes has been the development of the internet. Although many South Sudanese are still cut off from those changes, there is a growing awareness of that electronic world. How about you? Are you on social media where people can follow and contact you? Do you have a website? Social media sites? Please share the links.

HTDM: Frankly speaking, I am a computer and technology illiterate because I did not do any course. All I know is just to open Facebook, send messages, or check emails, but the full knowledge of operating is still a challenge. To the people of South Sudan, of course, this technology goes with literacy. Since ninety percent of the South Sudanese population are still illiterate, the use of the internet or other forms of technology, especially their use of applications, is limited. We tried to go for e-government functions, but it became difficult in the states because many officials do not know how to operate the technology.

RM: Any plan of writing a book to share your experiences and knowledge with the next generations?

HTDM: Yes, it is my dream. But I have not fully and finally decided to do so. It is in my plan, and I am still collecting the data.

RM: Any plan or dream of running the higher of office?

HTDM: No. not right now, and maybe later on. Because now, I am in my early 60's, maybe in my 70's and if have chance to do so.

RM: What's your current assignment in the R-Transitional Government of the National Unity?

HTDM: I don't have an assignment yet. But I will let you know if I am given a job.

RM: Why did you resign from your party, "the National Congress Party?"

HTDM: Like I said in the previous question that I was appointed a Deputy Speaker to the Regional Assembly of Southern Sudan by President Bashir and seconded by President Kiir. However, such a position was not stipulated in the CPA. But the SPLM and because of the partnership in the Unity government with the NCP, the SPLM required to be given the Deputy Speaker in the National Assembly. Also, the NCP demanded the position of Deputy Speaker of the regional Assembly by then Southern Sudan. So, we swapped; Honorable Atem

Garang de Kuek went to the National Assembly from the SPLM as a Deputy Speaker, and I came to Southern Sudan's Assembly as a Deputy Speaker from the NCP. I was the deputy of Comrade James Wani Igga, who was then the Speaker, and Honorable Wani was the one who helped to establish the Assembly. I stayed there in the Assembly from 2005-2007; I decided to resign from the NCP because I was not happy with two things:

One, the NCP wanted me to speak ill about the Abyei. They wanted me to promote their agenda by convincing Southerners that Abyei belongs to the North, which undermines the interest of Abyei as our people. Because the Abyei people and the land both belong to South Sudan, it undermines the interest and brotherhood of South Sudanese with the people of Abyei.

Second, I wasn't even talking, and although I did like to bring the issue of Abyei to be discussed. I was not included in the committee or the political body that was tasked to monitor the peace implementation. However, I was the senior officer representing the NCP in the Government of South Sudan. I was given a platform then I could handle some cases in South Sudan with the leadership of the SPLM in Juba, but the NCP preferred their people from Northern Sudan to take up the brief concerning Abyei's issue Southern Sudanese were left out. So, we didn't have much say in the matter of Abyei.

**RM:** Maybe, the Northerner NCP members don't want you to negotiate with your people on their behalf? Because you might sympathize with your people and give up too significant concessions?

**HTDM:** Yes, that was the case; they thought I would compromise with my people. But to stay where people are always suspicious of you and doubt your actions, you don't feel comfortable. So, in 2007 I decided to resign. So, I called a press conference, and with me in the press conference, Comrade Malik Agar, Comrade Yasir Said Armani, and Comrade Pagan Amun. I made the statement at the meeting that I resigned officially.

**RM:** What was the reaction from President Bashir?

**HTDM:** Well, not President Bashir alone, but almost the whole NCP leadership was shocked. Because they were looking at me as one of their stronger NCP's South Sudanese leaders, that's why since in 1998, I didn't remain in just one position because I was moved from one place to another. So, they were shocked, and they tried to persuade me, but I told them it was too late and I had already made up my mind and had taken a decision.

**RM:** You made up your mind and decided to resign from your political party, which had entrusted you with a powerful position in South Sudan, and you still relinquish. Does this not fit into what the Northerners used to say, «Southerners are decent intellectuals at day time, but at night they are rebels?

**HTDM:** Well, these were things; it was a culture developed during the struggle. The orientation was that the South Sudanese inside were Islamized, and yes, some people joined Islam. But people went as far as to the point where they said that "for the Arabs to make sure that you have to be stamped on your buttock if you become a Muslim."

**RM:** Was it that real, or was it just a defamatory conspiracy?

**HTDM:** It could be a conspiracy. It was a way of discrediting, degrading, and diminishing people's images so that your people look at you as if you were an enemy. But, unfortunately, up to now, some of the senior members still have the mentality that those who came from the National Congress Party and even including people from the Diaspora, who came from the battlefields, believed the movement had been hijacked by those who came from the NCP and the Diaspora.

**RM:** SPLA/M is an organization that neglects its kids and raises, hugging, kissing, and even feeding others' children. Have you ever heard that song by Larson Angok?

**HTDM:** Larson Angok forgot himself. This was the saying that SPLM always failed its children and hugged and kissed the children of others; that statement came from the late Gen. Lual Diing Wol or Baba Africa. During the fight for liberation, some leaders left the movement off and on, running outside and back to the movement. They were always welcomed back. So, Larson's song is based on that saying of Lualdit, but when it comes to himself, to Larson Angok, if you ask him, were you involved in the SPLA? The answer is that he was with us in Khartoum and not in the SPLA/M. When we were appointed, he was the one who always conducted the welcoming parties. He sang so many songs for us and celebrated our appointments. So, he was one of us from Khartoum. If it is true that the SPLM hugged and embraced the children of others, then he was one of the children of the other.

**RM:** Economics is crucial to any country. You are aware of when oil was discovered. Today, oil is still a significant contributor to our country's economy. However, we need to develop other industries and resources. What suggestions would you make about the directions Juba should take?

**HTDM:** Yes. In the first place, South Sudan is a country endowed by God with so many resources. It is a resource-rich country but has not been exploited up to now. We are coming to the oil. Oil is a non-renewable resource. So, we have to diversify our production and our source of revenues by using the proceeds from oil such that we have non-oil generating revenues. From 2005 up to 2021, we never paid attention, but now we have deep major concerns for diversifying production and boosting government services.

**RM:** When I was a boy, I crossed the Jonglei Canal on my way to Ethiopia. Unfortunately, the canal has never been completed. Do you think that it might still be a partial solution both to the flooding in South Sudan and to improve our relationships with Sudan and Egypt?

**HTDM:** It is currently a point of discussion, but most people are against it because they don't benefit from it. First of all, we have the biggest sudd in the region and the world. He is here within Jonglei, and if Jonglei Canal is dug, the Sudd area will dry up, and it may be a desert. A flood is not a disaster to us. It has been living with us for centuries. Is it not a disaster, but the flood is a blessing because it brings fish and grasses for cattle to graze. Does our livelihood depend on it? There is no way we can allow our water to flow Egypt, and then our cattle which are the source of our livelihood would die of neglect. Yes, we can cooperate with Egyptians just like Ethiopia.

**RM:** What do you predict about South Sudan's relationship with her other neighbors? Do you see our region of Africa finding more and more in common, or perhaps divisions, especially about religion or political philosophies, drive the various nations apart?

**HTDM:** We have already taken steps toward being together. We are full members of the East African Community, and even our people are now in the East Africa Community Assembly. Still, some leaders of the East African Community are pushing for more union, eventually unity. But for the time being, let us have economic cooperation, and at the end of the economic cooperation, we can determine if we move toward complete unity. The fact is that some countries are poor they don't have reserves to back up their currencies. So, we told them, we were like the European Union, where every country is almost decadent, and their money is substantial then we could make a union, but for the time being, let us deal in the areas of customs and free border movements.

**RM:** Let's talk about sectarian fighting in South Sudan and Warrap state. To be specific, what could you do differently to reduce violence in Warrap State if you were reappointed as the Governor?

**HTDM:** I had this experience when I was a governor of Warrap state in 2008. There was a feud fighting between Aguok and Apuk, so I made a dialogue approach. I approached the chiefs and leaders of Gelweng, cattle camp youths, women, and especially the spear masters who had to audacity to bless the children when they carried out the fighting. I made a big conference, and I decided to take back the authority of the chiefs. Now, you can see those red uniforms of the leaders. I was the one who introduced those uniforms because I said to make chiefs feel powerful and part and partial to the system, they must be given two things: first, they must have uniforms and caps similar to district-administrator officers; Second, they must be paid a salary. Each of them was getting one thousand South Sudanese Pound. "You being the government employee, you must be in charge of your duties because to whom much is given, much is requested."

Giving them uniforms distinguished their titles, the color and the description of their uniforms for both the executive chiefs and subchiefs: red scarf for executive chefs and subchief wear a black scarf. Now, it is easier the dismissal those who commit crimes. Because when you stripped off the chief of his uniforms and the people learn that he had been relieved of his assignment, the chiefs should avoid or prevent this situation. They start to work hard to follow the government's line and carry out the direct orders properly, especially in keeping laws and mandates.

I held a conference in Tonj, and it was attended by the President, whereby they reconciled before the President. The blessing water was brought, but the President said he didn't want the spear master to bless the reconciliation. But instead, he wanted the elders' women whose husbands died because of the hands for these people to take char-

ge of the blessing. So, we called Mama Ayen Park, the widow of late William Deng Nhial, and Mama Nyandeng Kuerbino, the widow of late Kuerbino Kuanyin Bol, to spray the reconciling communities with the water of blessing.

The societies were peaceful until I left, and there were no fights. So, when I left, I was succeeded by a female governor Madam Nyandeng Malek. There were several issues: First, all the Tonj resolutions of reconciliations were put aside, and they were not followed; second, there was no engagement of the chiefs anymore.

They don't meet with the governor. However, the chiefs have a forum, Council of the Traditional Authority Leaders COTAL, which I formed when I was governor. In that COTAL, they met annually. The governor must meet with them bi-annually or once a year at the COTAL headquarters. They have not engaged anymore, and their salaries were not given to them anymore. They were canceled on the pretext that "Tor knew where he was bringing this money, but I don't know where this money came from." It was the same money for security that I was using to pay the chiefs instead of improving my lifestyle.

**RM:** So, do you think engaging the traditional authorities could be the better solution for resolving that violence among the cattle-raiding communities?

**HTDM:** These raiding cattle people, especially the Dinka and Nuer, don't believe in violence or force and anything forced on them. So, they say let it be; they also retaliate and confront you, but when you dialogue with them seriously and break it down to them why violence is unnecessary, they will understand. Especially when a Dinka person tells you, "That person defeated me with his words," he is convinced. Therefore, he will not create a problem again, which will build trust between the people. But confrontation will perpetuate the cycle of violence.

**RM:** Do you think that someday Sudan and South Sudan may re-unite or perhaps develop some form of a special relationship? But, for that to happen, what would have to change in both countries?

**HTDM:** No. This thing of the reunion is out of the question. But we deserve in the long run is the cooperation between the two countries, especially in the area of security because north and South Sudan have the longest border. The proper security arrangement along the border will be a priority, especially by not allowing the dissent insurgents from either to go to the other country for political refuge and then arrange and launch an attack from the other country. If it happens, it must be stopped, allowing the smooth movement of people and goods and services between two countries because all of us have interests. South Sudan is interested because its oil passes through Khartoum to the Red Sea, and for Khartoum, South Sudan is its biggest market, especially the northern part of South Sudan. Almost five states of South Sudan shared a border with Sudan.

**RM:** What are your thoughts on Abyei?

**HTDM:** Abyei's people and land belong to South Sudan. It was only taken administratively and annexed to Kordofan in 1905. The reasons were obvious; the colonial power was looking for resources. There was this thing called poll taxes where they taxed people or households. They would pick one person from the family to be the taxpayer, or that was rotated among the family—you pay this year, and somebody else from the family will pay next.

There were no roads in 1905, but there were heavy rains and floods almost every year when this poll tax money was taken to the headquarters in Wau. It was a long way from Abyei; to ease the process, the money was redirected through Kordofan, El Obeid, which was a shorter distance and to which transportation was more readily available. That decision was the main reason Abyei was annexed administratively to El Obeid. It was not because of the land or especially the people.

When we, South Sudan, claimed Abyei back, it was given to us after the arbitrations in The Hague. The court acknowledged that the administration of Abyei and its nine Dinka Ngok chiefdoms belong to South Sudan. That's what we have been after, that Abyei must come back to us. What complicated things more was the discovery of the oil in Abyei. It is the oil that has made the Abyei situation so tricky. Since most oil deposits were discovered in South Sudan, the North wanted to hold on to Abyei to take advantage of South Sudan's resources.

**RM:** How many times have you been the Governor of Warrap State? When was the first you were appointed?

**HTDM:** I have been a governor of Warrap States three-time: First, I was appointed governor in 2002 to replace Machar Achiek Adaria, and then I was relieved; later on, 2004, when there was a general cease-fire, I was reappointed as a governor until we were relieved by the Dr. John Garang when the CPA was signed; the third time I was reappointed governor was in 2008-2010 under the leadership of the SPLM, but when people were getting ready for the 2010 general election.

The Political Bureau decided to form a committee in all states of South Sudan to scrutinize and screen all the candidates for the gubernatorial elections and because of some conspiracies led by some senior politicians in the national government and especially, there were some members of the Political Bureau who played a negative role by influencing those committees during the scrutiny. As a governor, I was audited based on my performance. I was given an approvable rate of 100% in literacy and performance. Still, they realized that I would lead the candidates, which meant I would stay Governor of Warrap State—just like those of Governor Louis Lobong of Eastern Equatoria State. When the scrutiny and screening committee realized that, they gave me zero in popularity. They believed I was not popular and, therefore, a different candidate would be suitable to contest for the Governor of Warrap State.

Given zero in popularity and even though I was a governor! "Come on," I told them, "Why don't you at least give me one or two percent? But, of course, I cannot be zero in popularity when I have a wife, mother, children, relatives, friends, and even my governor staff, including my deputy governor, advisors, and ministers. Even a teacher cannot give you zero points on paper you didn't do anything on it; they might give you a point for writing your name and date on the top of the paper."

**RM:** Leadership at the Local level where young men are turned into politicians overnight, such as counties commissioners, and the conflict that rise between the traditional rulers and young politicians. What your take on this matter?

**HTDM:** Well, indeed, that was one of the great mistakes we committed. When I was in Khartoum in 1994—Sudan was redivided into 46 states. The central government was very mindful because they were not called counties; they were called localities, and localities are the level closest to the people. For instance, let us say Dinka, for example; we don't want to be tribalist, but let the Dinka society be an example in this scenario. In a Dinka tribe, when you send a young person to deliver a message to the older man, the older adult first will not give regard or consider the statement; second, he will see you or me as disrespecting him because why sending a boy or a young person. But if you send somebody who is almost his age or agemate, he will take the message seriously, and if he needs to ask you something, he will ask you later on. But for us here, we think giving these people positions of County Commissioners is a good fit for the young person because it is where people think they will get better training, which is wrong and opposite. If you want to train them, then make them ministers, but take older people, retired gene-

rals from the Army, retired undersecretaries, and retired administrators, you take them to be the County Commissioners because they will command the respect of the communities and the people in that county, because of this entitlement of *Ngekdit*, *Ngekdit*, and *Ngekdit*, their word is adequately heard and abided by. Their orders are carried out.

In our community, age matters. When you take a young person to deal with an age-dominated society, age is a determining factor. So, when you take somebody who is almost a grandson of somebody, how can your grandson now be giving you commands, harassing you, and possibly he doesn't even speak to you with respect. This is why there is a setback. The political leaders let the young men do all they could, and that's why there were fights everywhere. After all, people are saying, "These are the young men who are fighting. How come? These young men who are fighting don't have parents?"

But we neglected the fact that young people listen to their parents and their chiefs. Still, they are not active because the situation had been left for these young politicians at the counties level to deal with the situation. The young people in the rural areas will look at the young man as their agemate, and they don't listen to him. They would say, "' Who he thinks he is? He was one of us recently, and who the hell he thinks he is now?"

**RM:** One primary source of hard currency in South Sudan is the remittances sent home by those of us living in the Diaspora. My family has asked me for money, and I sent it. Some of it to educate my nieces and nephews, some to build my house in the village, and some for my father so he can buy more cows. What do you think of those three things? Is there a better thing I can do with the money I am sending back to South Sudan? Are there better ways I could invest in my homeland?

**HTDM:** Well, first, the question of sending money back home? This process has not been organized or legalized, or does it have a legal provision for it? It is done individually without government control. For example, in Khartoum, there was something called Duanna Matterapin. The workers who left Sudan and went to work in the Gulf states, their remittances were remitted through the Central Bank and the Central Bank of Sudan, giving the family of those workers local currencies and adding that to the reserves of the country's foreign currencies. The same thing with Egypt and other countries.

But in the case of South Sudan and South Sudanese who are sending money back from aboard: those sending money back home were not allowed by law to go out of the country and work and send the money back. They were people like you who were sent by the Movement because you were too young to be in the army, too young to be fighting. Now you're growing up there and are working, so you send money back to your family individually whatever the reason—whether for them to buy more cows or buy something else to improve their lives. That money is your effort to fill the space that was supposed to be filled by you in the family if you were here. You were supposed to cultivate and do other duties. Instead, you left, and you are sending back money—something to compensate for your absence.

**RM:** What is the citizenship role of those living in Diaspora? Should we be voting in South Sudan's elections? Should we have dual citizenship?

HTDM: Coming to voting, it was in the Comprehensive Peace Agreement because people were looking for the opinions of all South Sudanese wherever they were: were they for session or unity of the country.

We have about four or five national elections: a presidential election, National Assembly, members of the Council of States, governors of ten states, state assembly members, seventy-nine county commissioners. This means seventy-nine ballots. You cannot carry all these aboard to look for South Sudanese. Perhaps for the presidential election only, but that is not provided in the constitution.

Second, regarding dual citizenship. This matter has not yet been addressed. We are currently drafting citizenship rules. A citizen defends their country's territory. If there is external aggression, they support the nation against that danger. A citizen pays taxes to the government to facilitate the work of the common good and the delivery of services. And the citizen is the one who votes. These three are the definitions of a citizen of any country.

When it comes to dual citizenship, especially most of you in Diaspora, you are citizens of your new countries. Some of you have served in the military. You take part in their elections. If you are a citizen of the U.S., you vote for the President of the United States. You may even belong to a political party.

When it comes to taxes, you pay taxes to the government of the country you live and work in.

So, now, we want balance. Yes, by birth, your origins are South Sudanese. Of course, your relatives and family are here, but you as an individual are an American. You see now? Did you get my point? It is going to be addressed legally, and I think before the election comes. Right now, we have American citizens in the National Assembly and the ministries here. However, they still vote in U.S. elections; either they go to the American Embassy here where they cast their votes or travel back to America to vote. Still, they are members of the Assembly.

**RM:** Finally, is there anything you would like to say to the people of South Sudan that I did not ask you?

**HTDM:** Not to ask something. But I just want to give my heartfelt greetings, passion, and love to all my brothers, sisters, sons, and daughters in the Diaspora to keep in their minds that there is a South Sudan home. They must hold their cards like other nationals do, as they have seen the Arabs do in the Western World. The Arabs are promoting their cultures; they are promoting the way they dress and how the girls cover their heads, eyes, faces even though the West is resisting them, but they are strong. Holding tight to their cultures, so basically, to their family ties: that is what I want to tell my people over there in the West.

We don't have this thing if a child reaches the age of eighteen, then they depart, that they are no longer your child if they become an adult. No, we don't have it here. We have family ties. Even if you are seventy-year-old, you still stay with your family. Even we, the educated elite of South Sudan, are still bound to our traditions. If you go home, even if you are President like Salva Kiir, the elders can still order you to sit down and listen to their words while you are sitting down. And a person could be a mate or lover, and the elders lecture you and could be the ones to decide your marriage.

The elders are the ones who have held on to the culture, and that's why now in communities—and especially the Dinka community—the divorces and separation are not a lot. Still, lately, divorces are more commonly happening. Still, most in the urban areas, but in the rural areas, it is difficult to divorce because family is made together by the girl's relatives and relatives of the boy. They are not free to get united in marriage and decide alone to disunite; dismantling the union between you and your husband or wife these are not easy and is unacceptable. So, we have to hold to our cultures to be a strong family, and the strong family always produces strong men who are assets to their communities.

RM: Thank you, Honorable Tor Deng Mawien, for taking the time to meet with us.

# ACHUEI BLUE-LIGHT FASHION

Achuei Blue-light Fashion outfit with an affordable price.
It's located at Kololo road near American residency.

Juba, South Sudan

# A Conversation with Deng Majok Chol

by Deng Mayik Atem and Kenneth Weene

*Ramciel Magazine recently sat down with Deng Majok Chol. Deng Chol is a graduate of Arizona State University, and later went on to earn an MBA from George Washington University, and Two-year MPA from Harvard University in Cambridge, Massachusetts. He is currently studying hydrology (PhD in Geography and the Environment) at Oxford University in England. He is from Duk County in Jonglei state, South Sudan. In fact, Deng village lies on both sides of the (incomplete) Jonglei Canal. His research topic is: South Sudan's lungs:* **sustaining the Sudd under climate and socio-economic change.**

**RM:** What is hydrology?

**DMC:** Hydrology is a branch of science that concerns the study of water and its properties as it exists naturally on earth and in the atmosphere, and especially how it moves in perpetual cycle. As you know, there is a great deal of water in South Sudan, and the particular interest are the great swamps, one of which we call the Sudd. So, hydrology is an important topic for our country as it encompasses water resources and environmental watersheds.

**RM:** You said swamps; isn't there just one Sudd?

**DMC:** No. There are three swamps, each with unique multiplicity of channels. Together they cover an area greater than the size of England. Our great swamps contain billions of gallons of water. The three great swamps are: 1) The Sudd Wetland of the Bahr el Jebel River system, 2) the Bahr el Ghazal Wetland of the Bahr el Ghazal River system, and 3) the Machar Marshes of the Baro-Akobo- Sobat Rver system. About half of South

Sudan's people live around the Sudd Basin, and over three-quarter of the country population live in the vicinity of these three swamps. They include members of many tribes: Anuak, Nuer, Shilluk, Dinka, Mundari, Murle, and other communities.

**RM:** Three huge Sudds, wouldn't it be a good idea to just drain these swamps?

**DMC:** Whoa! No. That water is an important national resource. These are unique geographic areas of enormous biological, social, and economic importance. Here, nature- wetlands, rivers, mashes, rains, animals, and plants give life. For many people it forms their way of live and it represents great wealth. These swamps are the basis for agriculture and potentially could make South Sudan the breadbasket of Eastern Africa. It represents more value than the oil, of which our country is so proud. In Egypt and Sudan, when one cloud forms above a city, population rush outside to worship it that it may condense into rain. South Sudan should be so tender with its blessings in the form of water.

**RM:** You mentioned the water forms the way of life for many people. Could you say more about that?

**DMC:** Many communities live in the Sudd Basin. As you know, there are there are two main seasons in South Sudan: wet and dry. Take or give one month, the wet season begins approximately about the end of April and lasts about the end of November, followed by dry season, and the cycle continues annually. One of the major sources of water in the Sudd Basin is rain. During the dry

seasons, a lot of water evaporates. Some, of course, is absorbed into the land. And some is lost through evapotranspiration: it is taken up by plants and then evaporates from their leaves. During the dry times, especially during droughts, the waters recede. Traditionally, many communities move with the water as their natural ability to navigates the area during hydrological imbalances. During the wet times, they would live on higher ground. When the droughts came, they would move closer to the water. This allowed them to grow different crops in the islands within the swamps. Also, fishing opportunities would change with the water depth. And, of course, wild animals would change their migratory patterns, particularly during dry times they would move close to the swamps so they could have reliable water supplies while they could roam more freely when there was a rainy season.

One thing to keep in mind is that those wild animals represent potentially huge tourism industry. South Sudan has a wonderful array of animals, and we need to develop tourism to bring in hard currency.

**RM:** So, you are saying there are dry/wet cycles that are important to the Sudd hydrology?

**DMC:** Yes, there is a cycle, but there have also been major periods of prolonged drought and heavy rainfall. One thing we need to study is the effect of climate change and variability on the hydrology and viability of these swamps. That is my major area of study, creating models that will better predict what future rains or lack of rains will do to our country. Right now, we have had some serious largescale flooding in the last 3 to 4 years at least in one of the three swamps, but we need to be thinking ahead as a country.

Another thing to remember is that flooding in one part of the country does not mean there is not a drought in areas at the same time. The models we use must consider not only the overall water cycle conditions for South Sudan, but the regional ones and they also must reflect what is happening in the rest of East Africa, particular in the Equatorial Lakes countries of Rwanda, Burundi, and Uganda. Remember that much of the water in our swamps comes from outside our boarders. One of the reasons we have so much water collecting in South Sudan is that we have extensive low-lying and flat areas in which the water can collect. Also, in most areas we have clay soil which means less rate of infiltration of the water into the ground.

RM: Given that we have so much water, why do you consider it so valuable?

DMC: First, South Sudan does not have too much water; the country simply does not have a sustainable water resources management plan or strategies to that end. The Sudd and its water resources, if managed properly, could be the greatest economic asset of South Sudan, even more precious and economically rewarding than the country's unstable petroleum sector. It is also valuable because there are other countries that need water. Sudan and Egypt need that water, especially as Ethiopia fills the lake behind its Renaissance Dam. So, the water has immediate value to those two countries. That was why the Jonglei Canal was originally proposed in 1904. Remember, one of the reasons that South Sudanese wanted independence was because they felt that Khartoum regime was stealing our resources. Beyond that, water is key to agriculture. If we can develop ways to storage water while opening fields throughout what is now swampland, we can become the breadbasket of East Africa. There are so many crops we could be growing, especially those which require lots of water like rice.

RM: Is the government in Juba working towards a cohesive water policy?

DMC: Of course, I am a student and not part of those discussions. There is a Ministry of Irrigation and Water Resources, which only came into existence soon after the independence in 2011. The United Nations emphasized the importance of the Sudd by designating 5,700,000 as Ramsar site (wetlands of international importance) in 2006. But I do not know the ministry has been considering the future of the Sudd or the effects of climate change on our water system. To the best of my knowledge, there are no university programs studying hydrology in South Sudan and no support for any students studying the subject in other countries. I must admit, I wish that the government in Juba were interested in supporting my research. However, I would also point out that research often supports the political point of view of those supporting it. That is why the scientists in Ethiopia and those in Egypt have reached such different positions about the potential effects of filling the Grand Ethiopian Renaissance Dam (GERD)

RM: If you were asked to help develop a policy for the Sudd, what are some of your thoughts on what it should include.

DMC: First, we must remember that millions of people live in those areas. We also need to remember the whole of the ecology, including marine life and especially our wild animals. To just go in and massively change things, even if you believe those changes could work, would endanger eons of human adaptation and animal evolution. Of course, we also need to recognize that things are already changing. For one thing, people have been clustering together in larger towns, although that really is not the right word since they often lack governance and infrastructure. People are gathering for two major reasons, the availability of trading—the material goods of the rest of the world are clearly shifting the subsistence lifestyles—and the availability of education for the children. In almost every such town there is at least a rudimentary school. It will take many years for the children of South Sudan to be universally literate, but South Sudanese parents want what is best for their children.

Another thing that is changing is quality of the water. One of my concerns is the effect of petroleum extraction on our water. Because oil offers immediate return, it is easy for politicians to put petroleum production ahead of water policy. That would be a major error.

But, back to your question. To truly develop the swamp areas, there will need to be new infrastructure not only handling and distributing the water but also roads for moving the agricultural products that could be raised on that reclaimed land and moving the goods and supplies that the people who would be living in those towns would need. And, of course, the housing and amenities of those communities would have to be developed.

There would be a tremendous need for technology and equipment. One of the most important things would be providing experts to assist those farmers and assistance to those farmers in obtaining the equipment they would need to raise cash crops.

Finally, there need to be proper governance at national, state, and local levels. The small villages that have historically been typical of the Sudd are based on a communal governance. Everybody might, for example, plant and harvest a field together. There is no individual ownership of those crops, although livestock are typically a different situation. How will ownership and the distribution of profits be organized in a more modern agricultural village? That is something that will require a good government or there will be too much friction. One of the most important goals of government- considering better understanding of the hydrology of the Sudd- should always be the resiliency of the local communities in the face of climatic change and variability.

RM: Do you have a parting observation you would like to make?

DMC: There is great diversity in South Sudan: ecological diversity and human diversity. We have 64 tribes in our country. How we share among ourselves, that we share among ourselves is crucial. We have had too much division. We need to find unity and common cause. Certainly, when it comes to developing what may be our greatest resource, our abundant water, we need to remember that fairness and sharing are essential if our country is to prosper.

# CLAIMING OUR SPOT ON THE COURT

Having defeated Mali (69-65) at the qualifiers for the FIBA Afro-Basketball tournament in Monastir, Tunisia, the South Sudan men's basketball team has given our people something to get excited about.

Thanks to their coach Luol Deng, who is an inspiration for us all, the team is making us proud. Given our recent history of internal strife and suffering, how wonderful it is to have reason to cheer. How wonderful it is to have a sports team that is flying our flag with true accomplishment.

As a nation, we need heroes who represent our future and we need to create shared stories that give us a sense of dignity and pride. Sports is certainly one area in which we can hope to achieve not just as individual athletes but as a society. Hopefully, our men's basketball team's success will bring us together across tribal and regional lines. Let us cheer as one nation and express our sense of pride and unity as we watch our team take their place on the court.

Hopefully, other teams will follow and hopefully the individual accomplishments of other South Sudanese will help us develop a national identity that will help us overcome divisions and help us become a better, a greater, and a more unified country and people.

# WHOSE NATIONAL ANTHEM?

By Deng Mayik Atem

T he recent visit of Vice-President H.E. Mama Rebecca Nyandeng de Mabior to speak on behalf of South Sudan at the United Nations General Assembly meant that she was also able to visit South Sudanese in Washington D.C, Omaha, Nebraska, and the Arizona South Sudanese community in Phoenix.

At the Omaha conference, there was some surprise that the national anthem of our homeland was not played. While Pastor John opened the conference with a heartfelt prayer that mentioned the words of that anthem and its references to God, the anthem was not heard. Most of us who attended figured that somebody had made a mistake.

No, they had not. As came to light when preparations were made for the Phoenix event, the Vice-President's protocol officer was instructing people that the national anthem "could be played only when the President of the Republic is present." Although playing the anthem was on the agenda for the reception, the organizers were told that was a "no-go zone."

The M.C. for the event, Deng Atem, complied with those instructions, but the omission did not pass without attention. Many of the children, who were to perform dances and songs in recognition of the Vice-President commented that somebody must have made a mistake. Then Mama Umjuma Deng was called to make her remarks. She demanded that the national anthem be played. "We are South Sudanese, and we are going to Celebrate our National Anthem," she exclaimed loudly.

To the Vice-President's credit, she recognized that playing the anthem was important to the attendees and she instructed the M.C. to have it played.

National symbols solidify the people's pride. The South Sudanese national anthem should not be appropriated to one individual, not even the nation's president. The recent visit of Vice-President H.E. Mama Rebecca Nyandeng de Mabior to Phoenix, was welcomed with joy by the Arizona South Sudanese Americans. It had been a long time since a high-level delegate from the government in Juba last visited Phoenix— six years ago, to be exact. Mama Rebecca's visit was a time to express our pride as South Sudanese. It was not a time for anyone to lay claim to our national song, not even Salva Kiir Mayardit.

On Sunday, October 10, 2021, the proper ownership of that anthem was clear; it belonged to Mama Umjuma Deng and to each and every one of us who loves South Sudan.

# A Conversation with Honorable Philip Jada Natana

By Ramciel Magazine's Deng Mayik Atem,
October 29, 2021.

*An Interview of the Honorable Philip Jada Natana, South Sudanese Ambassador to the United States.*

**RM:** Mr. Ambassador, as you know, Ramciel Magazine is trying to connect the people of South Sudan who are in the diaspora to one another and to the people back home. What do you think are some things that we in the diaspora could be doing to help our motherland better?

**HPJN:** When I got here to the United States in 2018, after being assigned as an ambassador, from day one, I said my role here, the first primary to focus on promoting and defending bilateral relations between the U.S. and South Sudan, but I think much more important is the issue of how much we can tap into the diaspora because, I considered our diaspora to be an asset that could be utilized for the development of our country for several reasons: First, coming from South Sudan. I think the good of our diaspora have opportunities they would not have had if they were still in South Sudan. Second, they are also exposed, and they could see how people live in diversity, and for example, here in America, there are many races from different countries. Third, they can practically see how hard people work here in America.

We could use all the skills, experience, and knowledge our people have acquired here and transfer it back home to help our nation. I have the feeling that as the South Sudanese diaspora living here in the United States, they have learned so much that they can take home and not only in terms of how people could be hardworking but

how people can live in harmony and try to tolerate each other in term of differences. But also, there are issues of good practices; you know when you talk about democracy and how we accept each other and try to create a favorable climate for everyone so they can have a say in the issues that matter to the people.

But much more important is the investment issue, so much that the diaspora can mobilize from the different spaces, people, or companies interested in investing in South Sudan. So, I think that there is so much the diaspora could do back in South Sudan.

**RM:** Follow-up question: How do we do that? How do the people live here in the diaspora and the rest of the west? How will they get those messages back home to South Sudan? That is part of the mission of Ramciel Magazine. What are some of the ways we in the diaspora could teach acceptance of diversity? What are some of the ways we can help model the value of hard work?

**HPJN:** That's an excellent question. They can do that practically in several ways: First, the people who are here in the diaspora are in constant communication with their families and friends back home, or in the area which are in the hot-spots, it only takes a phone call to reach those they had grown up with and say no this that is not the way you can do that. There are ways of treating each other. People in the diaspora have much influence among their relatives and friends back home, and people can listen to them. The second way of doing that is that people living here in the

diaspora often go back home, for many once or twice a year, and they spend a lot of time among their people in South Sudan enjoying holidays and making up lost time. When they go home, they can hang out with their families and friends from other tribes; that creates harmony. People could see that you are hanging out with the people of different tribes, which is a good thing. I think the only of teaching people back home about diversity is precisely by practically living it. There is always an opportunity when our people go back home, and I think they should focus on that and try to make the best use of it.

**RM:** Given the way our South Sudanese society is currently functioning, do you think that sending money back home—money that is often spent on buying electronics that can't be used, buying guns, and buying cows that only serve as a symbol of importance—is something we in the diaspora should be doing; or perhaps there are better ways

we could provide financial help to our families and friends to use the money more wisely?

**HPJN:** Well, I think what we need to adjust in terms of sending money. What you have said before about the money being misused and not being used for the right purpose, I agree with that. As the ambassador here, I get requests from people wanting an iPhone. I don't have one myself. I know that I don't need one; so, I have to say no to them.

There is no point in anyone buying such expensive electronics. You probably agree that some of those costly phones are on our young men and women who are not even working and earning a decent salary, and often those items are things we can't even afford here in the U.S.

Often people get money from a relative in the U.S.A. and feel they can spend it in any way they want. That attitude encourages wasteful behaviors and buying things that are just supposed to enhance your prestige, things like an iPhone and, yes, the buying of cows.

When it comes to buying cows, I do think it could be used positively. Once they buy a cow, they need to be encouraged to move away from just keeping this cow from the thief. When I talk about sharing the experience or teaching of what has been learned in the diaspora, that would be one of the examples. Let's say I invest in cows back in South Sudan; I will have to hire somebody back there to take care of my cow. That becomes a form of employment. But, more importantly, what I want to do is go back once in a while and be able to sell those cows and turn my investment into something else.

We need to teach our people how to do business in new ways different from those rooted in our cultures. Let me give an example. During those days of liberation, I traveled to one of the towns in Northern Uganda on my way to Koboko. I saw all these traders carrying stuff like clothes and mats on their heads to go and sell it in South Sudan; they wanted to trade with one of the cattle-keeping tribes. I talked to one of the people from that area, a tribal man who happened to be working for an N.G.O. I said, "You know, why don't you start a conversation with these people and tell them that maybe five or six of them can contribute and buy a lorry to have something like a cooperative shop and take all these clothes and take it there and people will buy from it. Put money together and set up a shop?"

He said, "No, no, you are not thinking like our people. For us, money is a commodity for cows and not the way around. You cannot sell your cows to have money to buy a lorry." That is the reality which is, unfortunately, a profoundly rooted mentality, but it can change.

You know, it is not just in South Sudan; other societies value cows and sometimes other animals. But when you practically start showing them an example of how you can turn that into monetary

terms and you know having money that you can use to buy other things and invest in different ways, I think that will work, that their attitudes will change. But, again, I always emphasize the practical aspect of it because people can learn more by seeing it. So if they see me using buying and selling cows to get things they value, they will learn from that.

RM: Follow up question: One of the problems that exist is the cost of sending packages from the U.S. to South Sudan. Say a person wants to send things to their family back home to South Sudan from the United States, it costs so much to send then it becomes easier and less expensive to send money? Rather than just sending money, wouldn't it be better if we could send useful material things back home? Even if they then choose to sell those items, at least that would be encouraging an entrepreneurial outlook. Might it be helpful to work with the U.S. Postal Service to reduce the cost of mailing packages to South Sudan?

HPJN: Well, posting things to South Sudan is a great challenge as I speak to you now; there have been several offers, facemasks, and examples; there is a friend of mine who has an organization willing to help.

Some things need to be shipped, things which are lifesavers, such as medicines and foods, but the cost of transporting foods from the United States to South Sudan is an outrage. So, yes, I mean, we should be encouraging cooperation between the U.S. and South Sudanese postal services. The International Postal System exists to promote such collaboration, and South Sudan is a member of that organization. It is up to our minister of Transport and Communication to work with the I.P.S. There are already attempts by some individuals tracking and transporting to South Sudan. Still, we need the Government to do more.

The Government needs to work on our domestic postal service as well. Even now, most residents of Juba residences have an actual address.

However, often when people want to mail things to South Sudan, the recipients don't have an address or a phone number to be called and told to come to pick up their mail. Addressing this was a subject I discussed last month on the sidelines of the United Nations General Assembly. During that discussion, I talked about my experience in Eritrea and how their postal services were among the best in the continent. In Eritrea, even if you don't have any physical address and have left a telephone number, they will call you, and then you can pick it up. Also, you have the option of renting a mailbox within the post office.

These are things in my role as ambassador that I need to pick up with the minister of telecommunications and Postal Service. These things could be done quickly, and we don't need to wait; it makes it easier for those who want to send something back home, and it is even a revenue-generating activity for the Government.

RM: Let's switch to some domestic politics questions: Given the long animosity between the Dinka and the Nuer, do you think South Sudan can ever have internal peace? Do you think our country might have a better chance for peace if we turned to the other smaller tribes for leadership?

HPJN: Thank you very much for this very important question, because without peace you can't even think of development and all these other things people are sending money home for. When people are running for their lives, nothing works. Unfortunately, after independence and even before that, we have had several very distributing incidents happen between various tribes. You mentioned the Dinka and Nuer, but there has also been violence between other tribes in Upper Nile like Murle and tribes in Equatoria and Bahr El Ghazal. The violence has been widespread and quite disturbing. We have had violence between communities and in places that have never experienced such violence before.

Now, what is the way forward? One of the

things the Government has done, which I think is very good, was the establishment of the National Dialogue in South Sudan. This was the first-time people sat together as South Sudanese and tried to look at the things disturbing the country and talk them out. It went up from the grassroots level, and from there, people have been able to discuss their grudges and even look at the root causes of problems, ranging from cattle raiding and fighting over other resources. I think that process of the National Dialogue is something we should build on because it provides solutions that are coming from the people. It is always a mistake for the Government to determine what the people want instead of listening to the people. The Government and civilians should be partners. The National Dialogue process is essential if people are going to work together successfully.

Sadly, some people want to fish in dirty water; criminal elements do not want peace and reconciliation. For one reason or another, some people benefit from fighting and chaos. We in the Government have to enhance and build the capacity for those who are supposed to be working towards peace without fear. Those who initiate criminal activities must be brought to book, and the law enforced. Until that happens, people who feel they can get away with committing crimes and violence will continue.

At the same time, we look at the solution from the grassroots level by having the Dialogue, and the Government will have to deal with those who break the laws and sanction them accordingly.

**RM:** Is the Government arguing against the weapons embargo by saying they need new weapons to create a joint force to maintain the peace? What do you think about the need to import more weapons into South Sudan; why can't the guns already in the hands of the Dinka and Nuer militias be used? There are way too many guns already in use in South Sudan?

**HPJN:** I think that is an excellent question, but at the same time, it is a tricky question. Still, I believe there has to be, for instance, the peace agreement stipulated that all armed forces should come to the containment areas where they are supposed to reorganize and retrain and then become one national army for the nation. But, unfortunately, most of the forces from the armed rebel group fighting the Government showed up at the training camps without any weapons at all. And I think that process ought to start over. I know that people are negotiating about it.

For us to have an organized army that would carry out any reform we want, we need to say, "It is okay if you want to be a part of the army. You are telling us that you have been part of the rebels' forces before. You weren't fighting with a stick; you were fighting with a gun, so show up with your weapon, or we are not just going to take you in to be part of the army."

By the way, one of the tasks that the organized army is supposed to be fulfilling is disarmament, collecting guns from the civilian population. For me, they should not just be collected, but we must also do something with them. Because if you order them and just put them in storage, one way or another, they will find their way back to the streets into the of the same people. I think that it is a priority for the Government to take measures towards disarmament. This process had already started around the area like in Tonj, Warrap state, and the other regions, and I think it should be expanded to other places.

You mentioned that "the Government is complaining that lack of the armaments is one of the challenges is not graduating the army was the lack of the armaments? Well, some of the armaments had gone to the population. The challenges are that the same weapons the civilians have are the same weapon the Government has, so the army doesn't have the kind of superiority in weapons it needs to complete its mission. It is kind of a catch 22 situation, we don't need more weapons, but at the same time, the army needs new and better guns. Some people say, "There should be an arms embargo that will reduce the violence," But you know, I don't much subscribe to that as a final solution. It could be a temporary solution that could hold for a while. Still, at the end of the day, if you don't address the root cause of the problems, whether there are arms in the hands of the civilians or not, if the root causes of our internal conflicts are not addressed, then the people will continue to fight. We have seen that in Rwanda, where more than a million people were killed in a short time by using guns. That's something that needs to be discussed very seriously, identifying and reducing those root causes?

RM: We have a follow-up question regarding the current sectional fighting among the Dinka in Warrap state, especially in Tonj east. Can the Government buy back the weapons from the civilians as one of the mechanisms of disarming civilians?

HPJN: Well, the issue of weapons in the hands of the people is a significant one, not only in South Sudan but even here in the United States. People consider it their right to possess arms, but how do they remove them. How do you navigate between responsible people who choose to have arms and those who will not use them responsibly? That is the biggest question that needs to be addressed. Of course, there will always be some voices on both sides.

Regarding your question, should the Government encourage buying back arms from the people who possess them? I don't think that will be the answer. Why do I say that? When you open up something like that, as I mentioned earlier, I worry about how all these guns came to be owned in the first place.

I will tell you from my experience as being part of the SPLA—and this goes back to the 1990s in the areas of Kapoeta, Yei, and the other regions where a lot of armaments were captured—the SPLA and S.P.L.M. then used to mark the weapons

that they used, mainly Ak.47s. When they found a G-3 rifle or guns like that, they didn't want them because they didn't want to look like a militia; everyone should be carrying the same weapon. Those weapons that had no use were traded for money, cows, or gold, especially in the area of Kapoeta. So, there was already an element of trading armaments that was cultivated in the people's hearts. If you now say let's go and buy the weapons from them, you are encouraging spread. You might buy them, but people will sneak them away, and again, and again you will have to buy them. So, I think what we need to do is come very strongly and say, "Okay, if you have guns, they need to be registered, and that way, you can determine who is supposed to possess the weapon." We need to have some supervision of weapons.

Authorities have to know who owns and who is responsible for a weapon. We need to ask, "What purpose do you want that weapon for?" But again, this comes back to the issue of security. Many people in South Sudan don't believe that Government can protect its people. That is the reason they give for acquiring weapons. I think the Government has to reassure people that the Government's job is to protect them. To do that, the Government has to have the ability to deal with any imminent danger, internal or external.

Talking about external threats, the army must be able to create protective zones in which we have sufficient strength not only to protect our people but also to punish any aggressor who tries to disturb our way of life. That has been done in neighboring countries; for instance, I remember Uganda did this among the Karamoja tribe. That "burn zone" approach is also why there have been no cases of significant cattle raiding since 1993 between Toposa in South Sudan and Turkana in Kenya. The people in charge of the army in the areas around Lokichogio and Kapoeta agreed on a mechanism to protect the people and their property. Providing such security is doable, but people have to move a little bit more aggressively as they go.

**RM:** Turning to U.S.—South Sudan Relations, there is a growing reluctance in the United States to give financial assistance to South Sudan? What do you think will have to change in South Sudan to make the United States perhaps more willing to be open-handed?

**HPJN:** We value our relationship with the United States. The United States has been an important ally that contributed in so many ways to the independence of South Sudan and continues to contribute to this day. We value our relationship and respect it. But I think the relationship between our countries can become a challenge because, for a very long time, the U.S. has believed that we have squandered a lot of the money we received from Washington and the rest of the international community.

Now, your question is, "How do we change that so the U.S. can continue to give?

First of all—and this is my personal view—I don't believe in Aid. I believe in trade. There is a lot of dignity when you trade. But if you only depend on Aid, then you are creating an imbalanced situation. The other day, the U.S. assistant secretary for Africa, Mary Phee, had a meeting with African's core diplomatic delegations. I attended that meeting and was pleased with the way that she started. She said we have to change the way that we conduct affairs. She emphasized that the U.S. does not see us as objects but as being in a partnership. That will result in mutual respect. We want South Sudan to be in such a partnership. Now, how do you do that when you are not bringing anything to the table? When are you always on the receiving end of Aid?

I think there is an excellent possibility that the U.S. can work with South Sudan, and we have already started. The current situation in the Horn of Africa, especially with Ethiopia, now Sudan, and we don't know how the case will turn out tomorrow in Sudan? They ask for one million men, and we don't see how the security officers will react? Tensions between Egypt and Ethiopia

and an upcoming election in Kenya, and you don't know which way people will vote? This is a deteriorating situation that we are dealing with. I think what South Sudan needs to do, and it has already been doing it, is contribute and try to mediate by enforcing the peace in the region. And, we had done that already, for example, when South Sudan brokered accords for Khartoum and various rebel groups.

Partnerships are what we South Sudanese want. I remember this word from our late leader, Dr. John Garang. "You know, in this world, you are not helping because you are helpless; you are helping because you can bring something to the table?" So, I think it is high time that we also talk about our contribution and what we can bring up to the table and in that way if the U.S. see that we can be instrumental in the region, they would be more open; but if we are there waiting for a hand-out then they can say whatever they want to say, and we will have no say whatsoever in this relationship. That is how I see it.

**RM:** Has the Government in Juba considered approaching American businesses to help grow our nation? If so, can you tell us what discussions are underway?

**HPJN:** Well, we have done. The business sectors here in the U.S. are based on the people, the Government might encourage, but they don't directly make people go and invest in a country A or B. The decision to invest will be based on the climate and conditions that are created; that is first. The second consideration is the issues that we are dealing with, especially the individual sanction that targeted individuals in South Sudan and then the subject of the arms embargo. The general advisory that had been put out by the U.S.—especially if you look at the website of the State Department's general advisory on traveling to South Sudan—is labeled #4, which means do not travel to South Sudan.

As to the Government, yes, we have tried to approach the business communities here in

the United States. In 2019, I remember we had something we called the roadshow. We organized a business week here in Washington D.C. in which we invited people to come and meet with us. We had a number of the ministers from South Sudan, such as ministers of finance, investment, agriculture, and foreign affairs. We created this forum to bring together members of the business communities and engage them in offering opportunities for doing business with us. That was one attempt we did at the level of the embassy. Even last week, I was in Salt Lake City. I had a perfect meeting with the Salt Lake City Chamber of Commerce, who brought some business people, and some of them are already doing business in South Sudan, although not on an enormous scale.

We are also part of the East African Community. Two-three weeks ago, a business meeting or symposium was organized by the East African Chamber of Commerce based in Dallas, Texas. I couldn't attend because I was engaged in business with Vice-President H.E. Mama Rebecca Nyandeng de Mabior, but we sent someone to represent us. I learned that the Ugandan Minister of Trade attended the event. This is the level of engagement we need, and of course, we are trying to approach American businesses individually. The process might be slow, but people are there. Just this morning, I received a call from someone who wants to invest in water in South Sudan. So, people like that are the people we want to work with. We believe that when we get these people on the ground and the message that will come out from them, we can hope it will encourage more people to invest.

Sometimes, you have an issue of perception whereby people will say that it is hazardous to do business in South Sudan and not just for Americans but even South Sudanese here. But we tell them, "Look here, we are making progress." We are not going to say that everything is okay and that the country is stable. There are challenges, but the people doing business in South Sudan are Ethiopians, Kenyans, Ugandans, Chinese, and many other nationalities. We advised them that there is a bit of instability but not all across the country. So, let's start where it is stable, and other less stable areas could see that, too. You know that there is an incentive to have peace; if this happens in this area because they are stable, maybe that will extend peace to others.

**RM:** If I hear you right? You are saying that the idea would be to get the people to come in and start doing business in stable areas because this success will help both spread the stability in South Sudan and encourage the other companies to come? This is a brilliant idea.

In many of the communities in South, Sudan men are willing to fight, but women are doing most of the work. When it comes to day-to-day work like farming, preparing food, taking care of clothes, and raising children, men traditionally have not done much of the work at all. What can be done to change that so that men have more of a work attitude? How can that change be brought about? Many South Sudanese men don't want to work; the women are far more willing to do jobs. The men want to sit around and talk and play their traditional roles. Then, if women work, the men want to use any money paid to their wives to buy cows. At least, that is certainly the case for the Dinka and Nuer.

**HPJN:** I think that can change, and I will give you an example; before the independence of South Sudan or even before the peace agreement was signed, there was a lady in Lake State who invested in farming, and she was in peanut farming, and her focus was using oxen. She started in a small way to do that farming, and her initiative was picked up by so many people. The initiative was started by

one of the N.G.O.s working in South Sudan, called Norwegian Aid. This Norwegian N.G.O. trains people in agriculture and farming, specifically farming using oxen and cattle. That training was done in many areas, and people started to see what that could do and start to pick it up.

My point is that the mentality of the people can only be changed if one of their own starts something, and they will believe in that. You know, my tribe does not keep cattle, so if I go and show up in cattle-keeping tribes and I say I will use their cows to farm, they will be offended. Because the cows were not supposed to misuse, and that constituted misuse if I did it. That goes with an old saying, "Change begins with yourself."

I think we should be having serious conservation of seeing that people who came from some of these areas should take the lead in contributing to a change of attitudes. Then, when they do the farming, their people will perceive them as if they were not looking down at the value of the cow but adding the value of the cow.

**RM:** Suppose an American farming company or a manufacturing company, whatever kind of a company it is, wants to invest in South Sudan. Is the Government in Juba prepared to say these are people from a particular community who would fit in nicely with your industry, and this is a place you should invest in training them? Are people from South Sudan different from those in the diaspora, or can they learn to work for money or industries bring some people and send them to the United States to learn these skills to come back to South Sudan. Do you think the Government can support this kind of idea?

**HPJN:** I think that would be something the Government would support. As I said earlier, our vice-president was here for the United Nations General Assembly meeting in New York. She told us about her own experience of getting her cows that produce milk, and people could see that. So, here is how we can make a difference.

But, of course, most of the cows and because of the method of grazing, the long distances, and so on, unfortunately, those cows are not very useful even for producing milk. But when you start introducing something that adds value, such as milk production, somebody adds money, and people could still keep their cows and have money from the milk they sell. So, things like that could add to the changing attitudes. I think I was giving you an example about the Norwegian People's Aid, an organization that went and brought people from Ethiopia, people who farm using cattle. And these people use local tools that can be used—not manufactured tools— but something that the local blacksmith could do.

First, what you do, you share the experience from the region. Second, have people who deal with the tools that are not sophisticated, not tools that might require being taken out of the area for maintenance. You can also contribute to your local area's economy because now, the local blacksmith who is in the area can work on those tools, and that's already an income. That process of inclusion could rotate around to everyone. Then, of course, we can build on that, and how do you build on that? Suppose there is a willingness of an N.G.O. or part of the Government or part of the farming industry to build the capacity to train the people. In that case, it is a practical aspect because it is a win-win situation for everybody.

**RM:** There are many questions about our country's relationships with the rest of Africa. Let's talk about two of them:

The first is water and water diplomacy. We in South Sudan have an excess of water; much of our country is flooded. Meanwhile, Egypt is desperately trying to shore up its water supply. How come we are not actively involved in diplomacy with Egypt to sell our excess water, deliver it by way of a canal or a pipeline to augment the flow of the Nile while Ethiopia fills behind its dam? Should we as a country be taking a much greater interest in hydrology?

**HPJN:** The issue of the water or the subject of the way is a politically continuous matter, especially to the downstream countries like Sudan and Egypt. Once we want to do something with the water, it immediately alerts them because they depend on the water for irrigation. Unfortunately, of course, South Sudan has not been able to use the water, especially the water of the Nile, to support our agriculture. Almost 100% of our agriculture depends on rainfall. I think the water is enough for all of us; it is only a question of management. Why do I say that? Because of all these conflicts we have had, especially the last war that lasted many years.

Like I said earlier, water is something very sensitive. I will give you an example; in 2017, in South Africa, there was a significant drought. Cape Town, in particular, and the rest of the Western Cape Province was running out of water. Everybody was desperate for water, and the Government had to look for the solution. The most interesting thing was that there were people who had privately owned water. They were farmers who had dug canals and small lakes that had collected water from the mountains, private lands, and farms. The Government wanted to use that water because of the shortage, but the owners said that they couldn't let the Government use their water freely and that the Government must pay if it wanted to use the water. And those created issues.

Many people in South Sudan do not want to share our water with other countries. Like those farmers in South Africa, they do not want to help others unless they are paid. They worry that someday we may need that water for ourselves.

**RM:** The second African issue we want to discuss is Sudan. First off, do you think the military junta now in power in Khartoum will respect the peace accord that was brokered with Juba and the various rebels? What do you think; will they go on the offensive against the former rebels who signed the peace with them, those in the Blue Nile, Nubia, and Darfur? And then we have Abyei. Again, do you think the junta will respect the agreement with Juba? If they don't respect the peace, what do you think Juba will do, again, especially if Khartoum goes on the military offensive in Abyei?

**HPJN:** The situation in Sudan is very worrying to those in the Government of South Sudan. It is not only because of the problems it makes for the people in Sudan but also because it might affect our oil revenues. We certainly want to have peace in Sudan before anything escalates. Our interest is that we need the stability of Sudan to resolve the crisis on the border and focus on the issues of Abyei. So far, the position that has been taken by the military as of this morning, especially in a statement by General Buhran, is that he is willing to work with the Prime Minister despite what has happened with the P.M. so far. That statement is an indication that all the pressures that have been coming from different parts, including the African Unions and the Security Council, are having an effect. Therefore, there is a suspicion that we will have a dialogue. We are trying to encourage that Dialogue because we don't want parties walking out of the coalition in Khartoum. But, of course, we continue to do our part, and so far, as you know, none of the rebel groups that signed the agreement have pulled out of the government agreements.

The Government of South Sudan encourages all these parties, especially the signatories to the agreement, that Dialogue must continue because we don't want this situation to be mishandled. Now, the position of the military leaders in Khartoum has been very clear. I think the African Union and the international community led by the United States plans to hold them to their words because they want to see a transition. After all, what was happening was that the country had almost been brought to its knee because of this disagreement between the coalition partners.

We need to do with neighboring countries and the international community to make sure that the Dialogue continues. Sudan is put back on its road to transition, which is the wish of the people of South Sudan. When we have a cooperative government in Sudan, it is easy for us to address the issues and the several proposals that that Government has forwarded. However, those proposals are still in the initial stage; they have been shared but not yet passed and put into effect. So, yes, there are still concerns. We are following the resolution in Khartoum carefully, and we are trying to see a positive solution that will satisfy all the sides that come out.

**RM:** Thank you, Mr. Ambassador, for taking the time to meet with us today.

# SSGE

ENTERTAINMENT

# THE SOUTH SUDANESE DIASPORA

By Ramciel Magazine's Deng Mayik Atem,

*An interview about the South Sudanese Diaspora, contributing to the development of South Sudan through business and skills, and knowledge transfer.*

*With Anjelo Malek Kuoc Deng, South Sudanese-American, Chief Administrative of Kush Petroleum Inc. and Owner of the Munuki Plaza.*

*Deng resettled to the United States in 2000, but after settling for a while, he decided to go back to his native land of South Sudan a month before South Sudan obtained its independence from Sudan in 2011.*

**RM:** What motivated you to return home?

**MKD:** First, let start by saying thanks for having me on your platform "Ramciel Magazine". Secondly, let me begin by saying as Diaspora, we have responsibilities toward our people and the country at large, there is a reason we are all over the world, it wasn't just coincidence. Our going into Diaspora has a very fine clear message behind it.

Some of our people were left behind during the arm's struggle to fight on our behalf, and we, as the Diaspora, who got lucky and a chance to resettle to the West, we were objectively hoping to get these Western, modern ideas and to come back to the motherland to make a difference when peace comes to our country. The idea was to come back and contribute to the development of our nation by using our skills, experiences, and the knowledge that we had gained in the Diaspora. Indeed, this was the shared goal between us and our western friends. Perhaps, some of us came back to South Sudan, and are currently playing a vital role in the nation-building. Although, we have faced so many challenges, still yet, this is a

home for us and one must confidently say we shall overcome the obstacles.

Just like those who had taken up arms, they have struggled and accomplished our goal. The road on our side was much more accessible. When I came back to South Sudan. I came having the concept that this is it. This is home! Overall, we the Diasporas have responsibilities to come back here and do something positive for generations to come.

**RM:** When did you go to the United States?

**MKD:** I went to the U.S. through Cairo, Egypt, on status of refugee and resettled in Salt Lake City in the State of Utah - December 2000. Long story short, it was like I didn't leave anything behind; our country was at war, and most of my siblings got scattered to unknown places and some joined the movement. And on a personal note, one must acknowledge that, God has blessed me with great opportunities in which I had accomplished admirable things while in the US, such as finishing my education, having good paying job and establishing family and of course buying a family house. Is like, I was leaving the American dreams! Those of us who were fortunate enough to go to America, Australia, Canada, and Europe had the opportunities to make sure we did what was best because we knew and we believed things were and could be possible.

When I went to the U.S. I put everything behind and focused on education and work. I achieved great things among the achievements, my undergraduate degree in international relations at The University of Utah and have some associates degrees in business management. While

pursuing that, I was working in the private sector; as a member of management and was holding title Shift manager at Wal Mart Stores Inc, USA, that way, I developed skills through several management trainings and more knowledge of running today daily business. I had started my MBA in 2007 at Strayer University in the State of Utah but I didn't finish it because I had to put off and focus on work as so I save up for my family when I come back to South Sudan. So, I came here, and got employed by Kush Petroleum, which was an opportunity accorded to me from the people that I admire the most, those of uncle Bona Panek Biar, Manasa Machar Bol and Kuer Dau Ding.

I was hired as one of the managements in the company, and along with that, I continue to pursue my master's degree in business school at Mount Kenya University through virtual distance learning, in which I completed in 2017, hopefully one day I shall pursue Ph.D. if time allows.

RM: Since you came here in 2011, you have done so much which could be inspirational for those in the Diaspora and a legacy for your children. Can you tell us how you balance the time between work here and with your family back in the United States?

MKD: I appreciate you asking this crucial question. Yes, I had been wanted to fit in somehow, but I could not find the channel to fit it in. And since you asked. Let me begin by using an old phrase that says something like this: "Behind every successful man, there is a strong woman." You know, I am blessed with a beautiful and strong woman Akuat Alor. If it wasn't for her, I wouldn't be here to manage all of this. Sincerely speaking, she stood behind me, and she has been managing the background taking care of our family back home in America.

In addition to that, she has been an important consultant all along, someone I seek the advice most of the time. So, yes, if it wasn't for her, I wouldn't have been able to help the family back home. I thank God for his gifts, for having her as my wife. We have been married for good 17 years and blessed with smart and health children. Indeed, she has been the ultimate guide and a big supporter to my success. One must say our love has grown better and richer over time. I love her more than I have ever loved anything (except God, of course).

So how do I manage it? Well, let me say I went to business schools, and obtained master's degree in business school. majored in Public Administration and Management. Prior to that, I worked in one of the giant retailers in America, I read some books; I learned from many writers and business owners I interacted with. So yes, it was not an easy task, but hey, so far, so good, I am managing…

On the family aspect, my wife and I, managed to put our two children to high school in the United States, and the rest of kids are progressing well and soon or latter they shall join others in the higher institution of learning. And while I am here, I have been managing my work to support my family. The progress is going on well in which I have started moving toward real-estate developing and at some point, God has blessed me with opportunities as I said earlier. Whereby I got the job and the people working in the field. These decent people help me come up with time to go back to the U.S. and visit my family and spend a little time with them and come back to continue the progress. We have never been disconnected. I thank God for the technology whereby one could talk to his kids through what I called 'The mother of FACETIME" and still being able to connect and give advises every time they try to slip away from the task. So, in reality, and in general, it is something doable.

I recommend everyone in the Diaspora to come back home and give a bit of sacrifice to our people and the country we all love. This is our land, and if we cannot do something here, our children may not be able to come back as we wish because they were born and grew up in that western lifestyle whereby, they may not want to live those western dreams. But if our children come back and find out we had established

something good for them, they can join our hands and live that dream as well as it has been my goal that, one day our children will come home.

RM: We are now on the fourth floor of this beautiful piece of real estate. Are you in the real estate business?

MKD: Well, yes. I am a business person. I do run a few businesses here and there, and I primarily focus on real estate development. So I seek to buy lands with little I have and develop it and move on at least this was what had wished and intended to continue doing.

RM: Why business rather than politics?

**MKD:** Well. Like I said earlier, this is a personal choice. I felt comfortable being in business rather in the government, but maybe someday if my people wishes I could help serve in the government, I will not hesitate to answer the call. But now I felt business is where I can progress and do what I do the best to contribute in the nation building.

So, I have been in the business for quite some time, and yes, some of us who came from the Diaspora and are here focusing on business and are doing okay. And that should be the message to the rest of our Diaspora to come back home and do the same because our country needs us. The country is still facing tremendous challenges due to the recent senseless war in 2013. Yet, we still believe and hope that, one day will think of the country and its people first than ourselves interest.

**RM:** How long did it take you to build the Munuki Plaza?

**MKD:** It was quite a struggle to set the records straight; I am not an engineer. I am a business-minded entrepreneur. Suppose you come and talk to me about business management. I will challenge you because that's what I had been doing for the last 20 years. The resources are always the key for every project you want to achieve. Having said so, I team-up with some friends to help with a little cash to start with. To mention my friend Mabior Chol who was the one I had started with his 60,000 South Sudanese pound which was equivalent to 15,000 USD in which I had been able to finished the foundation. Then comes in my friends Kezia and Asaga hebeab and among others. I had been able to work with the engineers, I think the amount of time it took was a bit longer than the normal time due to lack of resources. Indeed, I managed to complete in 2017 and grand opening was done in presence of my Mother Achol Yor, my wife Akuat Alor and our children who came from the US. We also had relatives and friends who came that day to witness the grand opening of Munuki Plaza! Indeed, it was unforgettable moments to me, friends, neighbors and the entire family.

**RM:** What's your advice to South Sudanese Youths?

MKD: I would advise them to focus on doing what is right and never take no as an answer to failure and should try to multitask in anything they do as so they can be an inspiration to others. Please don't sit back and watch others struggling to do great things for themselves when you are not part of it.

RM: Follow up question: You started early that behind a saucerful man is always a woman and your wife being an example of how she had managed and had done a lot to support you, especially by taking care of your children back in the United States, which afforded you flexibility and courage to come and do more thing here in South Sudan. What's your advice to the women of South Sudan?

MKD: My advice, you know, I take pride in a girl child education. Why? because educating the girl child produces mothers who are educated and will in return educate their children, care for their families and provide for their children. A girl child education prepares her to face realities in society and teaches her to be a good wife and mother. I give an example of my daughter Nyandeng which is now playing basketball in the U.S at her school Judge Memorial Catholic High School. And she is now in her eleven grades and she had been along good in both academically and in sports. One hopes that she could get the scholarship as she advances her educations. Also, among 37 children I brought from the village for schooling in Aweil city, among them there are quite a few girls, in fact 4 out of 10 are currently enrolled in high school and others are still in primary schools. As it said, "When You Educate a Girl, You Educate a Nation." – unknown.

So, my advice to our young women out there. Please, don't be discouraged. Maybe when I mentioned earlier that my wife takes care of our children and I am here in South Sudan, that doesn't mean that I have abandoned my wife so she could not follow her education. I am a good fan of a woman finishing her education. The only way you will pass on the message and shine as a young woman is to have an education and marry the right partner-in-crime. These are things young women need to hear:

1. Obtain an education.
2. Choose and marry the right partner, the earlier, the better, so you guys can grow together because you will be able to do many things.
3. Having children alone is also an education and progress in life.

As the Bible says, "Go forth and multiply and fill the earth."

**RM:** When you arrived in Juba. How was it, and how did you manage to overcome the challenges here?

**MKD:** It wasn't all by myself; I had people who helped me overcome some of the challenges. I have friends who came from the United States, people I already knew, and with whom I used to socialize. It wasn't that they were in a better position, but they had ideas, and they gave me a hand up. They wanted me to succeed, and I wanted them to grow as well. With the level of cooperation among us, we managed to lean each other and work cooperatively to achieve this Munuki Plaza. And, some of our friends have also achieved other little things on their own. And if I may mention one of the people that stood with me since the first day to have this place, it was my best friend, Mabior Chol Atem. So Mabior and I came a long way.

**RM:** Who's Mabior Chol Atem, and where is he now?

**MKD:** Mabior is one of the South Sudanese-Americans. He went to the United States in the mid-1990s as a young boy. He went to school, excelled, graduated with an MBA, and then returned to South Sudan, where he works in finance with one of the respected banks here in Juba. So, having good friends and people willing to offer the best advice is the key to success, and Mabior has shown me the way to do things right. In turn, I have shown some of my friends, even though I don't want to take credit for that.

**RM:** What other things have you done besides business so far?

**MKD:** Speaking of other things, not only focusing on trying to build ourselves, but my friends and I are also trying to build to the next generation of South Sudan. When I came back here in 2011, I had an idea whereby I felt like some people brought me up and America is one of the places that gave me a chance to become who I am. Let me put it point-blank so that I could be better understood. I came having an idea, and then I found out my brother General Dominic Deng Kuc had already started doing it. The idea was that he brought some children from the village to school in Kenya in 2007. And in 2012 I followed the same path, by sponsoring several children from the village to school in Aweil. And due to financial constraints, I couldn't take them to Kenya or any other part of the region. And since I had managed to build my father's house in Aweil, I decided to accommodate all those children there, and the progress and the transformation of these children is now moving on well, and among these thirty-seven children who are currently under my care and supervision, I hope next year we shall have more enrolled in the various high schools in Aweil State.

**RM:** Thank you, Mr. Anjelo Malek Kuc Deng, for taking the time to meet with us today.

# RAMICEL CELEBRATES A HEROINE MAMA REITA HUSTON OF PHOENIX, ARIZONA

By Ramciel Magazine's Madit R. Deng Yel & Deng Mayik Atern

*"Mama Reita is a true mother of the Lost Boys of Sudan. Since we made Phoenix our home, she has organized and celebrated our birthday parties and of course, she established the Gabriel's Dream Scholarship, from which I received assistance. I pray to God to bless her with more years so that she can see the fruits of her hard work."*

*(Panek Thii, Lost Boy of Sudan)*

As South Sudan struggled for its independence, many young people were trapped in camps, cut off from their homes and families. They became known as the Lost Boys of Sudan. A few were fortunate to be sent to the United States, and other Western countries, where they might further their education and have an opportunity for a normal life. However, it would be a life without connection to their homes. Thankfully, some people tried to fill that vacuum in their disrupted lives. Many were helped by aid agencies, teachers, employers, and foster parents. But, for those Lost Boys who ended up in Phoenix, Arizona, there was somebody else, somebody very special. That person was Reita Hutson, a woman whom the Lost Boys still call Mama Reita.

*"God had guided us into the hands of a woman who showed most of us the love and caring of a loving mother." (Malek Deng, Lostboy of Sudan)*

On July 20, 2020, Ramciel Magazine sat down with Mama Reita. Here is the interview:

**RM:** How are you doing?

**MR:** I still get up each day looking forward to what God has in store for me. It isn't as easy as it once was. My knee hurts and my back is a little weak. But I'm used to pushing my body. I was born during the Great Depression in a farming community in Ohio. Life on a farm back then was difficult, and it got a lot harder when Dad was called into the service. He was thirty-three and had three children, but the country needed him, so off he went to serve under General George Patton. My brother and I were very close, he must have been 9 and I was eight, but we did our best to help out; it was hard work. Our sister was just a few months old. We were renting a house on a farm that had no running water and Mom cooked on a wood-burning stove. We pumped in the water for cooking, laundry, cleaning, and drinking.

When I first got to know about Sudan, I talked with Gabriel and he told me about his life. It was funny how much we had in common, such as growing up on a farm. We both raised chickens for eating and eggs. We'd gather wood for the fire and pump water for drinking, laundry, and bathing. That water had to be brought into the house no matter what the weather. During the war, there was a garden to tend. You couldn't go into a store and buy much as there was rationing since most everything was going to the soldiers. So that garden was important. My family planted a big field of potatoes. Like Gabriel, we

did have to scare the birds off the garden so they wouldn't eat everything, and, of course, the girls helped their mommas with the cooking. There was a German farmer who lived down the road abd didn't have any children. I guess being German he wasn't much liked back then. My brother began following him around, and he taught him a lot including letting him drive his tractor and truck. Now, he's eighty-five and he's still farming. My brother is one of the most successful farmers in America. I guess you could say he and I grew up ambitious…and disciplined. In those days, you listened to your parents and grown-ups or your backside heard about it.

RM: Did you go to school?

MR: Oh, yes. Of course, it wasn't like schools nowadays. There were twelve grades all in one building. There was discipline at school, too. I was five when I started school and some students were

seventeen. But we all knew we were supposed to follow the rules. And, another thing, we were supposed to follow God and His teachings. We were introduced to God at school, and my mother made sure we said our prayers every night. We did not attend church on Sundays, but talking about God was still allowed in school so the teachers would tell us about Jesus and the Bible. We even had a weekly chapel meeting. When my father came back from Europe, there was something called the GI Bill and the government helped veterans buy houses. We bought a house in a town called Findlay, Ohio. I was in sixth grade then. I learned there was a church about a mile or two from our house, so I started walking to church twice a day. It wasn't just to pray but also for youth fellowship, and choir practice. That church became a second home to me even though my parents didn't go. I walked to church and I walked to school. Parents today do too much for their kids. When I was growing up we had to do a lot for ourselves and contribute at home. Today's parents aren't doing right by their children. Children have to learn to be responsible and disciplined. That's how I was raised and how I raised my children.

RM: How did you first hear of the Lost Boys of South Sudan?

MR: Well, the first time I heard of Sudan—of course, it was Sudan, not South Sudan—was watching television. I was living here in Scottsdale. There was a program called Touched by an Angel; it was very popular and I liked it because it was religious. One day, the story was about people being sold into slavery in Sudan. Wow! I didn't know there was slavery in this day and age. In the story, there was a young boy who wrote to his congresswoman and convinced her to help raise money for Sudan. Now, this was fictional TV, but it touched me. At the end of the show, Wayne Watson was singing "for such a time as this I was placed upon the earth to hear the voice of God and do his will." I felt like God was moving in me and wanted me to do something for the Sudanese. A week later, Tom Brokaw interviewed a man from Sudan; his name was Abraham Yel. He said something that I will never forget, "I am a lost boy in the world, but I am not lost from God." I wanted to reach out to him and to the other boys from Sudan, but my life was busy. I had grandchildren, children, friends, and a busy career as a Realtor. I didn't know much about using a computer, and there wasn't anything like Facebook or much social media. I read an article about the Sudanese living here in Phoenix and one day I saw a group of children playing in a park where I walked every day. They were with their Sunday School teacher. She told me. "These aren't Lost Boys. They live here with their parents." I saw more articles and I knew that God wanted me to do something, but I had no idea what. One Sunday I went to the grocery store and there was a tall, very black man who was standing by the maintenance closet. Something told me, "Oh, my God, this is one of

the Lost Boys." I introduced myself. He was very quiet, but he told me his name was Gabriel. Just like the angel. I thought, "God sent a young man bearing the name of an angel as confirmation to me."

RM: What has your relationship with Gabriel been?

MR: From that simple beginning, Gabriel became like a son to me. The relationship grew slowly and required a lot of getting past the differences in our views of the world. For example, one day I asked if he wanted to have something to eat. He looked as though he had been hit by lightning. I didn't understand his reaction until later when Gabriel came to my house and my family was there, including my son David who lives in Ohio. As we were eating dinner, David asked Gabriel, "Is this the first you ever ate with women?" Gabriel said it was. Little by little, Gabriel became part of our family. My eldest granddaughter was attending a Christian Academy in Scottsdale. I took Gabriel there to see a wonderful music production called Joseph and the Amazing Technicolor Dreamcoat. I loved how Gabriel reacted to the play. He called me Mom, the way my other children did. As I said, he became a member of our family. One day, just out of the blue, Gabriel said, "You know there are only two things I want, Mom: my education and my teeth." His lower front teeth had been knocked out during a rite of passage into manhood. When Gabriel told me that, I was flabbergasted. Such incredible differences between cultures! Among his people teeth were deliberately pulled, while we Americans spent fortunes on braces for our kids. Gabriel's simple wish started me thinking; What might I do to make a difference? That was the beginning of Gabriel's Dream, the non-profit organization I created to help him and other Lost Boys receive an education, dental and medical care. We did hundreds of other things, like helping with rent payments, car repairs, clothing, furniture, and more.

**RM:** Was Gabriel the only Lost Boy with whom you became close?

**MR:** Right after I met Gabriel, I met Jany Deng, a wonderfully outgoing young man, and Michael Lieh. They were doing fundraising for the Lost Boys' Center. I started volunteering at the Lost Boys' Center: showing Lost Boys how to write resumes, helping them find jobs, getting the simple things like toothbrushes and can openers, helping them with whatever I could like furnishing their apartments and getting my friends involved. My daughter, two of my friends from church and I decided to host the very first Easter for the Lost Boys, which we held at the Center. Of course, I didn't know Sudanese don't commit to things ahead of time, so I had a sign-up sheet. When I went back to the center and looked, there were only nine names. Still, we cooked a lot of food and hoped people would come. And low and behold, about 150 people showed up. My daughter, Julie, commented that it was like "the loaves and the fishes" because we had enough food. When we finished eating, Tut Gatyiel, the wonderful leader of the Lost Boys, gave a thank you speech. I cried while he spoke.

I had met a pastor at a Bible study, who was the minister at the big church in Paradise Valley. He invited me to speak at his church, and I brought Jany, Chol Jok, James Manyiel and several other Lost Boys with me. After the service, Dr. Bruce White, a dentist, gave me his card and offered to help. When I took Gabriel to see him, he offered a dental partial, which meant artificial teeth attached to Gabriel's teeth. I told Gabriel that was so nice, but if God willed, I would get him permanent implants. I had no idea how expensive implants were at the time. Later, Dr. White introduced me to a dental hygienist who volunteered at a dental clinic. She introduced me to a Jewish Dentist from South Africa, who volunteered to help Gabriel. It takes a long time to do implants, but eventually, Gabriel had his teeth. When other Lost Boys saw how Gabriel's teeth looked, they asked him if they could call me. I said, "Yes." So, that is how it began. Little did I know how monumental this project would become. I made their appointments and took every one of them to the dentist, and cared for each one at my home when they had surgery. Once they got the implants, then another dentist did the restorations, and if they needed fillings or cleanings, that required a different dentist. Some needed braces and wisdom teeth removed. Most of them required at least four to five dentists to fix their teeth problems. I had over one hundred of Phoenix's best dentists volunteer to help them. The dentists have told me that they do a lot of pro bono work, but the Lost Boys were the most appreciative of any and they loved helping them. So, Gabriel Kuany who also goes by Gabriel Chol Kuany was the first of my Lost Boys, but there have been many others. Gabriel and I visited my family in Cleveland in the summer of

2005. That meeting led my son David to help establish the Cleveland Lost Boys Association, and both he and my daughter Jennifer helped plan and cook meals like I was doing in Phoenix.

**RM:** What has given you the greatest sense of accomplishment in your work with the Lost Boys?

**MR:** Everything. (She laughs) I think the most important thing has been the work with education. I gave many young men scholarships. I raised most of the money through newsletters, and Gabriel and I spoke at churches and organizations. I also got a lot of support from Arizona State University, which provided scholarships to some of my boys. I was blessed to get three awards: The National Association of Realtors Good Neighbor Award, Arizona's coveted Hon Kachina Award, and a Worldwide Compassionate Award. Each award meant money for scholarships. My church, McDowell Mountain Community, also helped me monthly. But perhaps the best thing has been getting good medical and dental care for young men who needed it.

They weren't always Lost Boys. One time a Sudanese young man's sister called me. She said he was ill from a bad dental infection. I called one of the dentists and arranged for the sister to take him there. Later the dentist called and said, "You know, if you hadn't called me, this young man would have died because he had a bad infection that was traveling down his throat." Then there was Gabriel Lual. He asked Gabriel for my phone number and called me to ask for help. He had terrible headaches, and could not work. Since he was on the state-assisted medical insurance plan, he had just been given pain medications. I took him to a neurosurgeon who found a blood vessel pressing against his trigeminal nerve. He needed surgery, which solved the problem. While Gabriel was in surgery two of his relatives came from Tucson to pray with us and they stayed with me during the 7-hour surgery. Gabriel is healed!

Getting good dental care was so important for so many of the boys. It must have been terrifying the first time I took them to the dentist. Their only previous experience had been when their lower front teeth were painfully removed with hot metal as a rite of passage into manhood. I was amazed that they came with me so willingly, especially since many hardly knew me. And those dentists! What wonderful work they did! I began with just two, and they told other dentists. I recruited some through the Arizona Dental Association by setting up a booth for our program every year for four years at their annual convention. All of the dentists were listed as "Best Dentists" in the Phoenix Magazine. I got Lost Boys to also volunteer at the convention as I knew their presence would attract a lot of people.

**RM:** One of the most personal things you have done over the years is hold birthday parties for Lost Boys and Lost Girls even though most of them do not know their actual birthdays. Why did you do that? What makes those birthday celebrations important to you and them?

**MR:** I know that the Lost Boys and Girls don't know their actual birthdays. When their documents were created, they were assigned birthdays arbitrarily. Here in America, having a birthday party is one way parents tell their child that they are special. It's a way of saying, "This is your day." Well, I couldn't do that for the Lost Boys, but by holding one special birthday celebration for them it was my way of telling the entire South Sudanese community that they were special. It was always on January 1st as many were assigned that as their birthday in the refugee camp. Of course, we did Easter and Thanksgiving and first Sundays to help bring the community together, but somehow that annual birthday party said you guys are special, you are important to me, I love you. Sadly, I've had to cut back in the past few years. A Physical therapist injured my back and I had to stop. Still, I can look back on those celebrations and think

how joyous they were for me as well as for the South Sudanese and their friends who joined us. My volunteers and I loved doing it.

*"Around 2006, she started making appointments with the dentists to fix our teeth, and the funny thing she used to do? She admitted us at her house after the surgeries, so she could take care of us. She did that for every lost boy, and another thing Mama Reita used to do is celebrate our birthday every January 1 for the whole Sudanese community in Arizona. She also helps us with school tuition here in America and back home in South Sudan. Mama Reita was a gift to the lost boys and Sudanese community. May God keep blessing her for the outstanding and incredible job she had done for us. We will remember Mama Reita in our lifetime."*

*(John Nhial Pat, one of the Lost Boys of Sudan)*

**RM:** There must have been many people who helped you over the years.

**MR:** Too many to count, far too many to name. Doctors, dentists, lawyers, pastors, friends and family, and so many churches. Oh, the list goes on and on. I remember when Mayen Ayuel contacted me. His wife and baby were in Egypt. He said they had applied for a visa for his family to come. However, they were going to bring the wife and baby separately. I knew John McCain because I had volunteered in his office, so I helped Mayen write a letter to him seeking help. John made the arrangements for the wife and child to travel together. I guess people began to hear about me and see me as some sort of an expert on Sudan. Of course, I had never been to Africa, but I did care enough to keep trying to learn. After Mayen's wife and child arrived in Phoenix, she became pregnant. Sadly, they lost the baby, but then she started having other problems. She was admitted to the hospital, but they didn't understand what the hospital was telling them and they called me. The hospital did three MRIs and couldn't figure out what was wrong. I had read enough to suggest they look for parasites which they ultimately found in her brain. Thankfully, the treatment worked. After that, the hospital would call me about its patients from Sudan even though the HIPAA regulations said they couldn't. I helped get treatment for a lot of young men for parasites and for Trachoma, a disease that causes their eyelashes to scratch their eyes. I also found lawyers who volunteered to help them when they got into difficulty with the law.

**RM:** What do you think prepared you to do so much to help the Lost Boys of Sudan?

**MR:** First, my faith and the belief that God called me to help. Then, too, my childhood prepared me for a life of doing for others. Next, there is my love of hard work, something I learned as a child. When I was helping the Lost Boys, I often worked from 6 a.m. until 10 or 11p.m., seven days a week. I was 65 years old when I started helping, the age most people leave the workforce. I never got tired! My telephone rang all the time. I've also had a wonderful and fulfilling life as a mother and grandmother, and as a working woman. Along the way, my career has taught me how to communicate and how to reach out to those who can help.

I feel that all of my careers gave me the skills to be successful. I truly felt like God went before me opening the hearts of people to help, and it always seemed that a solution to a problem just came my way. I will never forget James Chan. I kept him several times overnight when he had dental surgery. The last time I kept him, I went outside with him to say goodbye. As we stood in my driveway, he said, "You know, this is the first time in my life I have known what it's like to have a mom." To have somebody who had been through what he had and to have him say that to me, it was a moment I will always cherish. None of what I did had anything to do with me. I was just the vessel. Like one of my friends said, "You made yourself available, you responded when God called."

**RM:** Many readers of Ramciel are going to college. Based on what you know of the Lost Boys, what advice can you give them?

**MR:** I don't think they need any advice from me. Gabriel often told me what life was like for him as a boy. Because there was no electricity, the family would sit and talk, learn all about their ancestors, the importance of the family and the village. I probably learned more from them than they learned from me. I think the strength they showed on their journey and in coming to a new country had to have come from their family, and life in the village and cattle camps. Somehow, I think that their life prepared them to walk thousands of miles, deal with terror, and survive when most of us would have perished. Many of our young people do not have the strength, the humility, good manners and respect for others and authority that I have seen in the Sudanese Lost Boys. In the face of adversity, the Lost Boys did not cry or give in. What was so amazing is that they never lost the joy of the Lord. Most of their employers told me they were the best workers they had ever had. They came with determination and they have put so much effort into their lives. They immediately wanted to start community college, and many of them are still in school working on advanced de-

grees. Some have doctorate degrees, some are in law school. I find it astounding how much they have accomplished, all without ever feeling sorry for themselves or complaining. If the young men and women of South Sudan want to know how to deal with the world, I suggest they look to the Lost Boys and how they have faced their lives, see how they have pressed on despite their circumstances and risen above them to achieve success.

*"The community of the Lost Boys of Sudan is so thankful to American volunteers like Mama Reita, for their unyielding support of our advocacy for peace in Sudan. Today, we are proud citizens of the Republic of South Sudan, which Reita supported vehemently."*

*(Deng Majok Chol, one of the lost boys of Sudan and Harvard Alumni)*

**RM:** Now that the Lost Boys and Girls of Sudan are grown into adults, is your work finished?

**MR:** Yes. I was forced to retire due to back and knee issues. However, before I retired, I teamed with a California surgeon, who had been to Sudan with Doctors Without Borders, and the two of us supported thirteen medical students, one of whom was a woman. We had to raise $100,000 a year. It was hard for me to do that because, during that time, I was injured in physical therapy and got a herniated disc. All of them have graduated, some have returned to Sudan, and one is doing his residency in Kenya. Eventually, I got a scholarship for future doctors for South Sudan. Gabriel's Dream was helping support these thirteen young men and one woman who were going to medical school in Kenya along with an organization known as Future Doctors for Sudan.

*"Mama Reita Huston became my direct sponsor and mentor. She has been able to sponsor my studies from the beginning of the third year from 2015 to 2017. During the sponsorship, there was timely payment of tuition fees and living expenses with studies running smoothly. I sincerely thank Mama Reita for helping me out during this difficult time. Her help has been invaluable, I don't know how I would have managed without her help and support. Because of her generosity I was able to complete medical studies and become a doctor."*

*(Dr. Elioba John Luate Raimon)*

**RM:** You have been receiving recognition for your work with the Lost Boys, for example, your appearance on the Queen Latifah show. How do you feel about such recognition?

**MR:** You know I wrote for a newspaper, I had a career in public relations, and produced some big events, so I knew how to get one's name into the news. If you Google my name, there are a lot of photos and articles, and I received several honors for my work that had a lot of news coverage. I was still a Realtor for the first few years when I started my foundation.

The National Association of Realtors and the State of Arizona gave me prestigious awards, so I wasn't surprised when the crew from the Queen Latifah show called me. There was a lot of interest in the movie the Good Lie, and I was happy to be on her show so that the world could see why I love these young men. Even though I was in pain from my back, I was happy to do the show, especially because it was going to be about the boys and the movie. I wanted the world to see why I love these young men. But I do admit that when there was so much love and appreciation shown to me and checks given to support our work… well, that was wonderful too.

*"Mom, your humbleness, kindness, and caring have given me footsteps to follow, and your love and support has given me wings to fly. You are the best Mom ever."*

*Gabriel Kuany*

S
C
O
O
P
S

Queen of Afrobeat Achuei Deng Ajing performing at the Miss &
Mr. Greater Bahr El Ghazal at the Freedom Hall edian Atongoya

South Sudan Basketball star: Christina Deng

Comedian Atongoya

Gabriel Mabeny Kuot

S
C
O
O
P
S

S
C
O
O
P
S

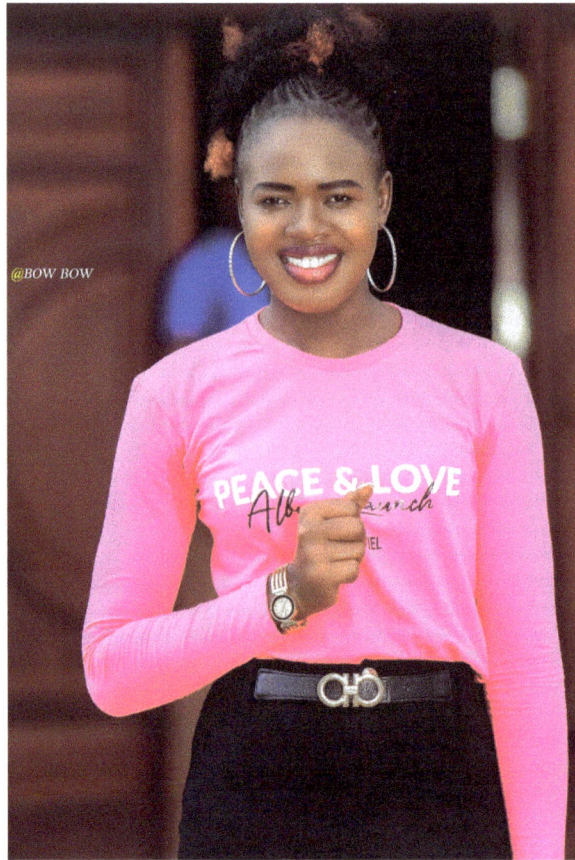

Aluel Manyiel Rou a.k.a. Lavala Vela
sporting her Peace & Love Album Launch T-shirt.

At Ramciel Magazine's dinner with the models and ambassadors.
Yier Bol, Peter Mawien, Mr. Bak, Gabriel Kuot, Mr. Robert, Deng Atem, and Eng. Chol

Duk woman's group performing
at the inauguration of Chief Aleer Gatluak Deng

Duk's Chief Aleer Gatluak Deng,
at a swearing-in ceremony in Western Australia

S
C
O
O
P
S

S
C
O
O
P
S

Alith Juach

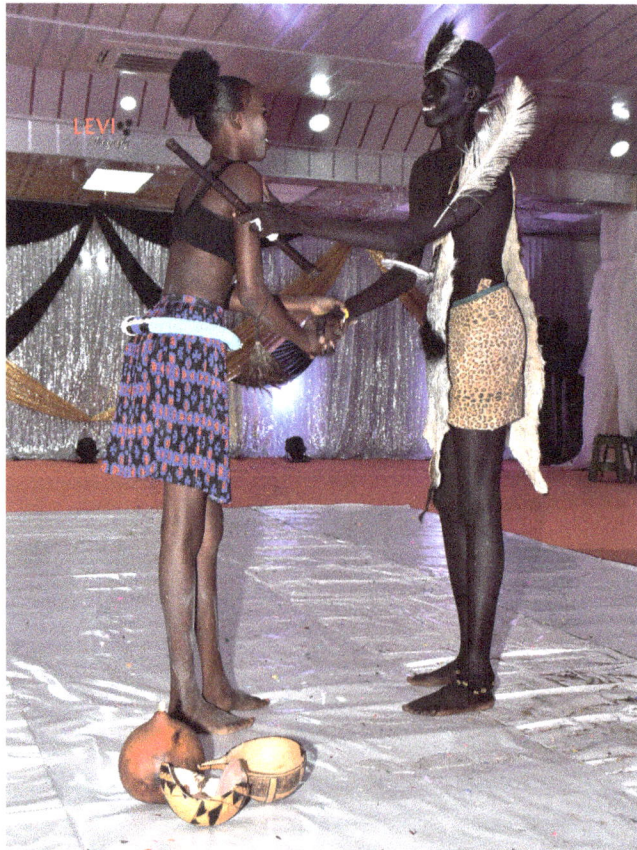

Zoyia Zoyia and her friend
during Miss and Mr. Greater Bahr el Ghazal

The winners of the Miss & Mr Greater Bahr El Ghazal beauty pageant were held in Freedom Hall in Juba on August 2, 2021. Queen Anoon Marial Deng and King Wol Khartoum.

*"Whatever mission you choose to accomplish, don't come back with empty hands. Fail and get up, try, and try!! Again, and again!! You are not destined to fail, but your persistence and hard work will make you reach your destiny of joy. Believe in yourself, and you will be someone. You're born to be somebody, so be you!*
*"Love and Peace are all we need."*

**King Wol Khartoum**
***Winner of Mr. Greater Bahr El Ghazal beauty pageant 2021***

S
C
O
O
P
S

Meet the musical Legend: Yaya Kuaja a.k.a Bol Kuaja. Songwriter, and one of the incredibly talented Artists who had cultivated his signature all over the Dinka culture.

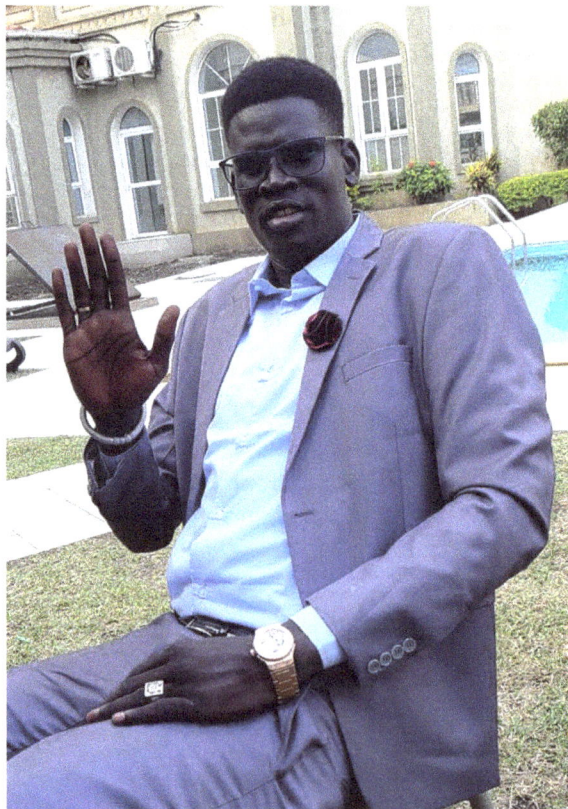

Kuaja started his music in 2006 and recorded his first album titled Junub Pelku Til in 2016. So far, he has had several hit songs, including Nyantoung Abyei and Nyan Wut Chier. If you love music. Follow Yaya Kuaja. His beautiful music resonated with all ages.

John Akuot Aciek, President of South Sudan Community Association of Western Australia, Majok Jawat Malek, Chairperson of Twi East Community Association of Western Australia, and Acting Chief of Twi East Peter Lual Reech Deng, witnessed the inauguration of Sultan Aleer Galtuak Deng Athoi's inauguration the first South Sudanese man to be a chief of the Diaspora in Australia.

*Sultan Aleer Galtuak Deng Athoi & Majok Jawat Malek,*
*Chairperson of TECAWA*

*We launched the Twi East Woman's uniform under the able leadership of the Chairlady under Nyankiir Garang Dual and chairperson, James Malou Atem*

# THE LAUNCH OF TWIC EAST
# WOMEN'S UNIFORM
# IN WESTERN AUSTRALIA (TECA WA INC.)

The Twic East Women in Western Australia under the able leadership of Nyankiir Garang Dual and Adut Khot Goch launched the first ever Twic East women uniform in Diaspora on 28th April 2019. The launch was spectacular and was attended by over 500 people. The launch generated thousands of dollars for the community. Nyankiir Garang Dual has been a valuable member for TECA WA Inc. She had served Twic East Community at various capacities since she came to Australia in 2005. The Twic East Bird (Stork/Arialbeek) represent Twic East values of integrity, honesty, respect, humility, resiliency and perseverance. The Twic East bird is a community's brand and logo. It is a responsibility of every Twic East member to promote it in one way or another.

Twic East community Association of Western Australia Inc. is one of the thriving South Sudanese communities in Western Australia. It was formed in 2004 with the main objective of helping Twic East community members to settle in a new country and to keep her members socially engaged. The TECA WA Inc. has been growing from strength to strength since its formation.

TECA WA Inc. had been instrumental in the formation of Twic East community Association of Australia (TECAA) in 2016. TECA WA Inc. hosted the Twic East global conference in 2017 which was attended by Twic East members across Australia and invited guests overseas. The dignitaries that attended the conference include current Twic East paramount chief Manyok Ajak Majok, former Twic East county commissioner Dau Akoi Jurkuch, current Vice President Rebecca Nyandeng De Mabior, Emeritus Bishop of Twic East Diocese His lordship Ezekiel Diing Ajang de Malangdit and many others. The TECA WA Inc. was the first South Sudanese communities in WA to have over $100, 000.00 in her account. The TECAA Inc. used TECA WA Inc. account as a guarantor for Twic East overseas dignitaries to visit Australia.

The secret for TECA WA Inc. resilience lies in the commitment of her members. The association has been peacefully transitioning from one leader to another since 2004. Chronologically, the leaders that presided over TECA WA Inc. are: Isaiah Ajang Reech Gak, Akech Dau Angok, Manyang Deng Biaar, Akim Buol Jok, James Malou Atem Ayiik, John Majok Jawat Malek and current chairperson Chol Rieh Garang.

On October 16, 2021, South Sudan Twic Mayardit Community of Arizona Honored and Celebrated Doug and Helen Grimwood for their extraordinary contributions to our community and our Center. Over the years, Doug and Helen have taken children from our communities to so many beautiful places, whether to play sports at YMCA, visit the Zoo, and even go camping. When we look back at the things, they had done for all of us, the kids they helped, the time they spent with the people in trouble, the legal advice they gave for Pro-bono, the way they been there for the people when they been scared and worried. I just wanted to say that they are so special. There aren't a lot of people in the world like the two. Tonight's celebration was just a token of our appreciation for all they had done. They have helped not only the lost boys and girls of Sudan but the entire Sudanese community. They had established a foundation that educated about 80 students, and over $315,000 in Scholarships to those students.

*~Marko Malong Atem Jok (Chairman of Arizona Twic Mayardit Community )*

*Front row: Doug Grimwood, Helen Grimwood, and Susan Edwards*
*Back row: Lynn Boddy, David Grimwood, Christi Grimwood, Minerva Grimwood, and Eugene Grimwood*

# Book Review

This book is about four sets of experiences in the liberation struggle of the people of South Sudan covering the period 1965 to 2005. The writer is Francis Deng who has served as diplomat for South Sudan at the UN and authored many publications covering this and related topics. The individuals whose stories are narrated in this volume include one man, three women, and a child of nine years at the time of documented experience. All five individuals hailed from the Ngok Dinka tribe of Abyei which is a province sandwiched between North and South Sudan but is culturally and racially Southern. The theme of the book is rebellion against perceived injustice and the different paths chosen to resist oppression and support the aggrieved people of South Sudan. The man, Pieng Deng Kuol, was a brilliant student of engineering in the University of Khartoum. He established and managed a camp for unaccompanied children that became an internationally acclaimed success, and many were resettled in the United States, Canada, Australia and elsewhere. They became well known worldwide as the Lost Boys (later, Boys and Girls) who, to this day, revere Pieng as their Father and Leader. Pieng went on from there to distinguish himself as a remarkable commander in the military struggle for independence of South Sudan and later as chief of police. Pieng's half-sister Awuor Deng, who was later joined by her sister, also called Awuor, was motivated to join the rebellion by the humiliation she suffered as a Southern Sudanese student in the Junior Secondary School in Khartoum. The third story is that of Nyenagwek Kuol who found herself struggling within the system, but in which she paradoxically found opportunities to serve her people, including by redeeming abducted children and returning them to their families. The fourth story in this compilation tells the same saga from the perspective of a child, Raphael Tikley Abiem, who was driven to rebel by raging anger against injustice, mistreatment and intolerable indignity, by joining the Anya-Nya armed liberation struggle (1955-1972) at the tender age of nine years.

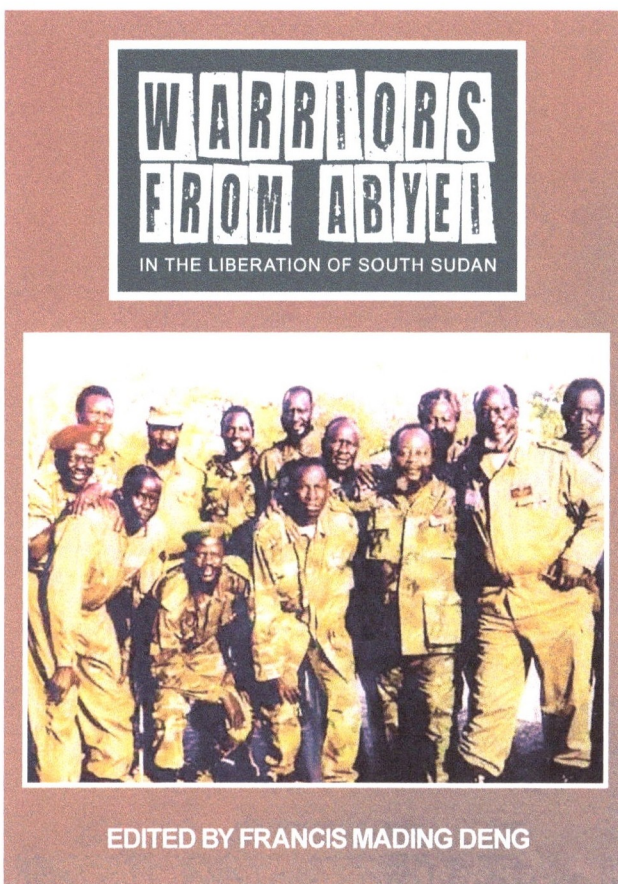

The individual stories are told in the first person in the words of the protagonists with commentary and analysis provided by the author. There are many close encounters with danger and the possibility of sudden death haunts each of the narratives. There is no mistaking whose side the author, Francis Deng is on, but he attempts to understand the general problem of conflict resolution from a political and academic perspective in the final part of the book. The question is, given that differences are sure to arise between neighboring peoples and countries, how to avoid violence and resolve conflicts peacefully. Sudan in recent times has paid a heavy price. I would recommend this book to anyone interested in the history of the modern liberation struggle of South Sudan with a particular emphasis on the human toll.

*Paul George*

# BOOK REVIEW

The debut non-fiction book from the very successful Dr. Jacob Dut Chol Riak, South Sudan State Formation: Failures, Shocks and Hopes, is a well-researched and informative piece of literature that details the many facets that have helped contribute (or be the detriment of) the development and formation of the South Sudan State. It also details and encompasses the aspects of South Sudanese society that have prevented the country from progressing, as well as the raw tenacity and hope that the citizens have for their home-country. As someone that is not from South Sudan and was completely unaware of the political strife and tension occurring in the state, I found this book extremely insightful and thought-provoking, each chapter increasing my knowledge on the politics and the crises occurring in pre and current South Sudan.

The book is broken down into ten separate and distinct chapters that encompass South Sudan's state formation. Dr. Riak has provided thorough and wonderful context about the historical and modern theories of state formation, giving a fantastic academic background for his discussions on South Sudanese politics, economics, social attributes and militaristic insights. It is clear that Dr. Riak has undertaken a massive amount of research to give his book true authenticity and intelligence. He provides an almost insane number of sources that give credibility to his statements and facts; I trust what he says and explains.

My favourite aspect of this book has to be the obvious passion Dr. Riak has for this topic. From his very informative style of writing to his lengthy analyses of subjects, such as the numerous theories and perspectives he delves into and the role that the Troika countries play in South Sudanese politics, it is clear that Dr. Riak has enjoyed writing and researching this book. There is also a huge emphasis on explaining and elaborating aspects and definitions in the book, which are helpful. In particular, its section dedicated to the numerous abbreviations and acronyms he uses is intricate yet easy to read, and being able to read the book with that information ready is very handy. It is plain to see that Dr. Riak has implemented an overwhelming amount of care for this work, and it shines through.

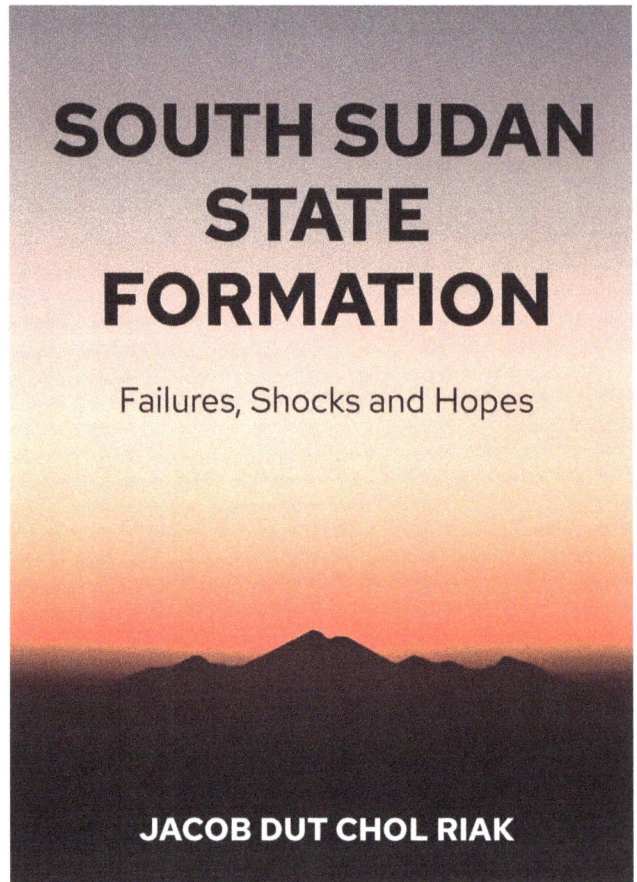

I also enjoy the topics that he raises in his book. While often bleak and straight-to--the-point about the negative aspects surrounding South Sudan, Dr. Riak also offers glimmers of hope in his writing, showing alternate perspectives often when talking about catastrophic events and battles, such as the 15th December Political Crisis.

Whether you're an outsider to South Sudan who just wants to learn more, or a South Sudanese citizen or researcher who wants to learn about their country, Dr. Riak's South Sudan State Formation: Failures, Shocks and Hopes is an in-depth choice that will help you understand all of the political strife that has occurred, consolidated into a single 400-page book. I believe that it is an essential book to have if you are invested in African politics. Rating: 9/10.

*Tyler Fleming*

# BOOK REVIEW

Not being familiar with Sudan, South Sudan or Sudanese culture before reading this book, it was daunting to write a review of such an eminent scholar and human rights advocate. I had some frame of reference, having lived in neighbouring Uganda previously; having worked with refugees for more than 20 years – as well as being Muslim and having married cross culturally myself. However, reading the Invisible Bridge was an unexpected gift.

It is a deeply personal account of the early life and formative years of the author, Dr Francis Mading Deng, as well as a detailed introduction - an autoethnography if you will, of the Dinka peoples, through the recall of his life experiences.

The author describes navigating the challenging landscape of being born the son of a widely influential and prominent chief, into a household dominated by the overarching personality and presence of his father who exerted control over some 200 wives, extended family networks and kinship ties.

The author constantly demonstrates and yearns not just for approval but expressions of love from a distant and intimidating, powerful father and key role model, trying to live up to the expectations (both explicit and implicit) of the family and himself.

He demonstrates a flair for mediation from a young age, whether on behalf of a transgressive and alienated brother in line for succession, with a prejudiced Italian neighbour, with the chair of the international student association in West Germany, or with strict headmasters on behalf of politically active fellow students.

Not one to shy away from speaking up in overwhelming situations and possibly put forward unpopular or unwelcome views, this is clearly the training ground of a successful career in the UN. Towards the end of the book, we have the example of the author having to delicately tiptoe around and sometimes firmly negotiate with an inexperienced yet zealous and heavy-handed military officer in charge of security forces.

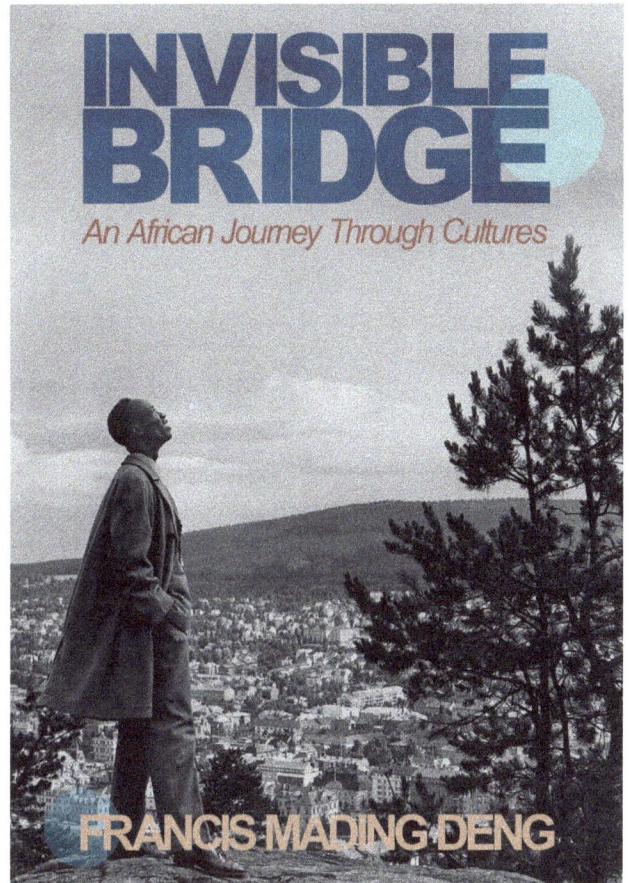

The author is surprisingly forward thinking and cosmopolitan by nature, and we follow his education around the globe which takes him to many places, including (former) East and West Germany, Italy, England and then the US, all the while attracted by a modernity new places have to offer. He experiences culture shock or crisis of faith, interestingly, not on first arrival in Germany, his first time in Europe, but in England - on threat of exile.

Aptly named Invisible Bridge: An African Journey Through Cultures, we follow author's path through education - both informal at the hands of parents, grandparents, traditional elders and extended family members - as well as formal institutions of the British administration and higher education in Khartoum and abroad.

The author was born in 1938, in a border area between the African South and Arab North of the former Republic of Sudan. He is Ngok Dinka - a people who, although identified as Southerners, were historically administered by a Northern province.

Traversing timelines and spanning across generations, the young Francis crosses at every point an invisible bridge to the next sphere of learning and influence, whether Christian or Muslim, North and South, East and West, traditional and modern - and also often crossing the distinctions between African, Arab and European. It begins where the long shadow of slavery still lingers in collective memory, on the cusp of nationalism and the independence movements which proceeded to sweep across North East Africa. It provides a glimpse into the political climate of the time - and foreshadows the tragic events to come.

We encounter these moments, his world, and the rites of passage that took him from the village near Abyei in Kordofan, all the way to New Haven in the US. While trying consciously to avoid over-sentimentality or nostalgia, it presents a view of home and homeland so clearly dear to him, as a legacy for others.

*Zheela Vokes*

### Moyi-be-dri-lata: A history of the Ma'di in South Sudan by Victor Keri Wani

This book is about the Ma'di, a Sudanese tribe who inhabit a vast area covering parts of South Sudan, Uganda and the Democratic Republic of Congo. The writer who hails from the region, draws on a variety of sources, not only academics who have studied the people, but eyewitnesses and the indigenous with specialized knowledge of particular events. He begins his account two thousand years before the first modern colonization, the Turco-Egyptian which took place in the 19th century. The book concludes with a discussion of border conflicts with neighbouring tribes and recommends a way forward for politicians to solve these disputes. It is a story that is complex and filled with human interest, a story about individuals, their successes and failures, their actions often governed by the desire for right to prevail or to redress perceived wrongs. If the conflict is not with other individuals or tribes, it is with wild

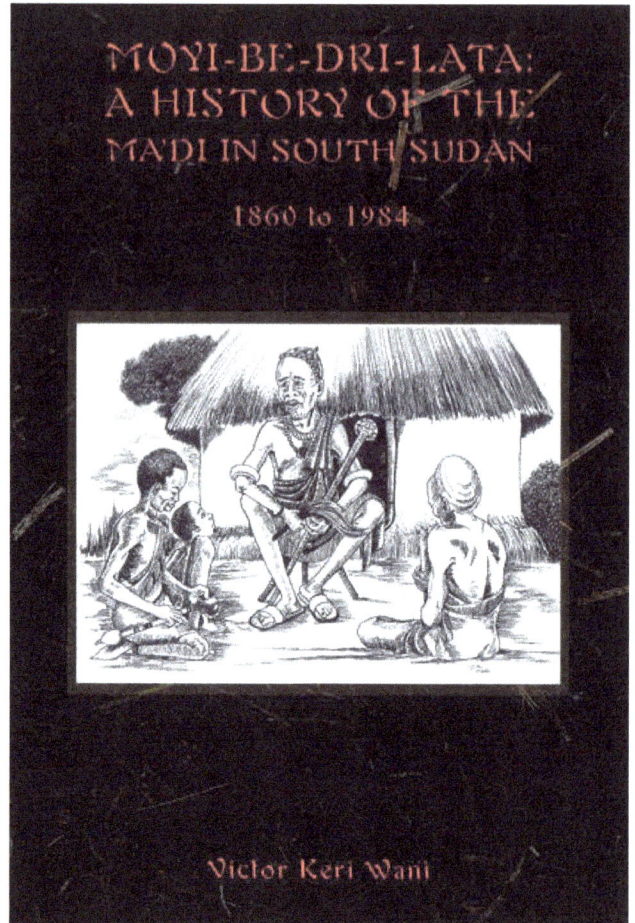

beasts or cloudless skies which bring devasting droughts requiring the services of the all-important rainmaker.

A glance at the table of contents shows a wide range of topics covered, including the migrations of the tribe, their traditional leaderships, clan structures, chief men and women, feuds, wars, religious beliefs, economics, education systems, traditions, relations with other Sudanese tribes and of course relations with the colonizers and the missionaries. The effect of modernization on the culture is also discussed. How the War of Independence affected the author personally is particularly moving.

I recommend this book to anyone who has an interest in authentic African history. It is written by an African who was oftentimes an eyewitness to the events he relates. It is suitable for the tertiary level as it is fully referenced or can be enjoyed by the general reader for the simple pleasure of learning about this unique people, and their message for humanity.

*Paul George, Perth, December 2021*

# IN MEMORIAM

Uncle Elijah Alier Ayom: a true hero of South Sudan has passed. Elijah, whom we who spent time in the Pinyudo Camp knew as Alier Ayom, was one of the camps elders and was responsible for the camp's financial and logistical operations. He was a quiet person given to speaking slowly. I remember how he would take a position at the center of the activity during ration distributions. Morning till night, he would make sure that children and others who were less able to fend for themselves were taken care of. In the evenings, he would turn on his radio so that we could hear of that great outside world of which we knew nothing.

When I picture Elijah in my mind, I see him carrying that radio and, of course, his calculator.

Often, we youngsters would be angry at Alier Ayom because there were things we wanted, particularly Diggig Papa, the sweet flour that was so easily cooked and so delicious. How childish it was of us. We did not understand that he could only distribute that which he had, that many items had to be shipped to the troops who were fighting for our cause, and that we had to make do. At times we would call him names and insist that he must be corrupt. How wrong that was. Elijah was an honest, dedicated, and hardworking man, a true servant of our cause.

Alier Ayom served in Ethiopia to the very end and was part of the evacuation. I saw him riding in a car towards the Gilo River. The car became mired in the mud, and Elijah, like the rest of us, continued the journey on foot and escaped back to our homeland without his possessions. I wonder if he was able to at least save that radio and his calculator.

So, another of the heroes of our independence has passed. At least his passing was in Juba, the capital of the nation he helped to birth. It cannot surprise us that the elders of our movement are dying. Not only are they old, but also, they have sacrificed so much in the battle. Still, it is sad to have those who meant so much in our youths die. I hope that Uncle Elijah Alier Ayom's family take comfort in what he has meant to our country and to those of us who were fortunate to have benefited from his careful stewardship at Pinyudo. May God rest his soul in peace

*~Deng Mayik Atem*

# WRITERS WRITING FELLOWSHIP
# SOUTH SUDAN

*Educate and Advocate with the PEN*

WWF was founded and championed by a group of South Sudanese Writers and Artists in different fields of Art. They desire to bring together an experienced team of writers that will nurture, coach, train and mentor, publish, and promote aspiring writers from South Sudan and give South Sudanese writers the platform to be heard and listened to as they share their experiences, and transfer writing life skills to aspiring writers for an intergenerational exchange of writing skills. WWF is part of the Board Leadership of South Sudan Youth Organizations Coalition.

Alith Cyer Mayar, founder of WWF, poet, writer, social entrepreneur, and author of The Cry of the South Sudanese Children and the Battle Within Me. "A friend told me, 'I wish to see South Sudanese writers have success stories among writers in the region and the world.' The power of our stories is something unique that only we can do best. I think it's about how our stories will bring back peace and heal the hurt."

WWF is championed by a team that works collaboratively:
Poet, Ngong Ngong (Truth Crisis) - Deputy Chair
Assunta Achol - General Secretary
Manelson Abraham - Finance

WWF can be contacted at:
alithstarlady@gmail.com

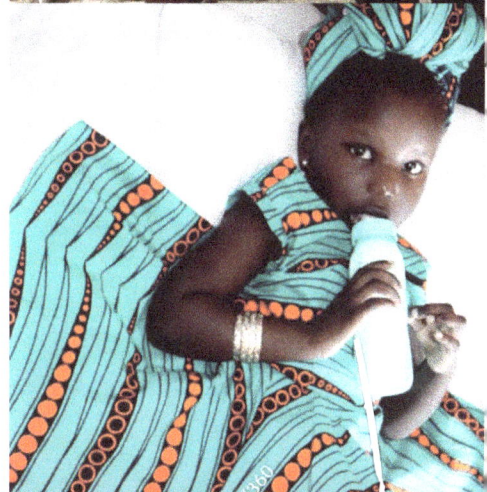

# EKON360 ARLINGTON TEXAS

A U.S. base Private
Custom Design Africans Wears made with sophisticated, high quality Africans
fabrics from the finest materials available.
Like our page to receive
the latest trends and updates

*Shop at www.ekon360.com*

## CHECK US OUT!  ALWAYS SOMETHING NEW!

Treat yourself to a well-deserved shopping spree, and fill your
closet with great fashion finds!

Africa World Books
Pty Ltd

www.ingramcontent.com/pod-product-compliance
Lightning Source LLC
Chambersburg PA
CBHW041621220326
41597CB00035BA/6189